Praise for *Here Be Dragons*

"*Here Be Dragons* is not just a hilarious book about parenting; it's a hopeful, honest, and wise book about becoming the grown-up you were always meant to be."

—Cecilia and Jason Hilkey, HappilyFamily.com

"Parenting is inherently funny and horrible and sweet and enervating and invigorating. Ken and Annmarie capture all of it. And they do so while writing beautifully and with real soul."

—Ken Kurson, Editor in Chief of the *New York Observer*

"*Here Be Dragons* proves that it is possible to raise children with both a sense of adventure and an obligation to serve others. Bravery and kindness are not mutually exclusive. Best of all, Ken and Annmarie show that parenting is a team sport. For anyone who doubts that building a family can indeed be a joyful journey, this book should be required reading."

—Eric Greitens, *New York Times* bestselling author of
The Heart and the Fist

)ks about parenting—about raising happy, successful, loving children. This is a book about raising children who are active citizens in a democracy—which, studies show, is more likely to make them happy, successful, and loving adults than almost anything else. Ken and Annmarie are American treasures; share their wealth of experience and wisdom."

—Joe Klein, author of *Charlie Mike* and *Primary Colors*

"I rarely read parenting books anymore. I find more guilt than freedom within most of their pages. But *Here Be Dragons* is different. I came away from Ken and Annmarie's memoir with a renewed vision of myself as a mom, and a rekindled appreciation for the adventures that have made up my own family's stories."

—Jamie C. Martin, author of *Give Your Child the World:*
Raising Globally Minded Kids One Book at a Time

"Ken and Annmarie are two very smart people who have written a very smart book on the many lessons that life has taught them about marriage, parenting, and trying to be good people. If you can handle blunt stories about barf, bedtime, poop, and tears, there's a lot to learn from this book."

—Rev. Damian J. Ference, Director of Human Formation,
Borromeo Seminary

"Equal parts humorous and heartbreaking, *Here Be Dragons* reminds us that although parenting isn't always a picnic, it doesn't have to feel like rat race. In reframing mishaps as adventures and reminding us all to take the time to change our socks, Ken and Annmarie provide both comic relief and solid advice for couples caught in the whirlwind that is parenting."

—Katie Hurley, LCSW, bestselling author of
The Happy Kid Handbook

"This hilarious account of one couple's parenting voyage illustrates how much more rewarding it can be to occasionally let go of the rudder and let the wind take the sails. Recommended for all high achievers who venture into parenting with the perfect plan only to find the baby barfed on your map."

—Kelly Watson, coauthor, *The Orange Line: A Woman's Guide to Integrating Career, Family and Life*

"Through their adventures in life-living and child-rearing, Ken and Annmarie demonstrate the humor, strength, and forgiveness necessary to strike a balance between the home front and the larger world. For anyone trying to navigate both work and family, the Harbaughs offer an amazing and hopeful perspective."

—Tracey Miller-Zarneke, coauthor of *Before Ever After: The Lost Lectures of Walt Disney's Animation Studio*

"Ken and Annmarie manage to be wise, funny, and relatable without being smug, superficial, or ordinary. Their journey from the parents they thought they would be to the parents they actually are is equal parts heartbreaking and hilarious. *Here Be Dragons* is a must-read for anyone looking to connect with the wonder—and wackiness—of being a mom or dad."

—Julie Fishman, coauthor of *The Little Black Book of Big Red Flags* and co-host of *First Timers*, a parenting podcast

HERE *be*
DRAGONS

FAMILIUS

Certain names and identifying characteristics have been changed, and certain events, especially the embarrassing ones, have been reordered and compressed.

Published by Familius LLC, www.familius.com

Familius books are available at special discounts for bulk purchases, whether for sales promotions or for family or corporate use. For more information, contact Familius Sales at 559-876-2170 or email orders@familius.com.

Library of Congress Cataloging-in-Publication Data
2016949869

Print ISBN 9781942934905
Ebook ISBN 9781944822293
Hardcover ISBN 9781944822309

Printed in the United States of America

Edited by Michele Robbins
Cover design by David Miles
Book design by Brooke Jorden

10 9 8 7 6 5 4 3 2 1
First Edition

HERE *be* DRAGONS

A PARENT'S GUIDE *to*

REDISCOVERING PURPOSE,

ADVENTURE, *and the*

UNFATHOMABLE

JOY OF THE JOURNEY

ANNMARIE KELLY-HARBAUGH AND KEN HARBAUGH

To our children, Katie, Lizzie, and Henry,
without whom this book would have
been finished much, much sooner.

Authors' Note

For whatever reason, books like this are often written from the viewpoint of one parent. We suspect that is because writing together causes entirely too many arguments. Neither of us is a solo act, so we have written this book as a team. We have lived together for almost twenty years and shared many of the same experiences. However, our interpretations of those events can be quite different. Plus, we found the repetition of the word "we" really annoying. Therefore, apart from the introduction and conclusion, which we narrate together, the rest of our stories are told from alternating perspectives.

Annmarie and Ken

Contents

Introduction:
We Used to Be Awesome

Niagara Falls was frozen. So were we. But we stood there anyway, the wind blowing through our coats and stinging our faces. Mom, Dad, two kids, and a baby gazing across the chasm at great vertical sheets of ice where the rushing water should have been. This was not the vacation we had envisioned. Our lives seemed as frozen as that waterfall.

We had health care, a new car, a great house, and a dog. But we were off kilter, disjointed, out of sync, and miserable. How had it come to this? We worked hard to afford our shared life, but we were not together often enough to enjoy it. The kids had grown accustomed to grumpy Mommy and AWOL Dad. Our lifestyle no longer seemed worth the sacrifice.

Before having children, we had been decent people. Interesting, even. One of us had taught Shakespeare to gang members, while the other flew reconnaissance missions off North Korea. One sailed across the Mediterranean Sea, and the other canoed the Suwannee River with ten troubled teenagers in tow. But our own children had proven our biggest challenge.

That weekend trip to Niagara was the closest thing to R&R that we'd had in months. We prepared the kids for a great natural wonder—the Cave of the Winds, the Maid of the Mist, the Aero Car suspended high above a tremendous whirlpool. But the waterfall was frozen and the tourist attractions were closed. As we stood alone on that ice-covered catwalk, which in warmer months hosted honeymooning couples from around the world, we realized something. Being married and building a family . . . at that moment, it kind of sucked.

Something had to change.

Purpose and Adventure

Children can break you. They grey your hair, try your patience, and ruin your weekly poker game. Sometimes it can be a challenge to remember what it was that prompted you to have kids in the first place. And work? Especially when we are providing for families, work becomes the thing we think we have to do to pay for the stuff we assume our family needs: dance classes, snowboarding camp, that summer cottage at the lake. No wonder most parents are exhausted.

We think there could be a better way. Maybe the key to maintaining both a happy family and a fulfilling career is to approach them with the intention of service and adventure. We are not the first folks to stumble upon this notion of serving others—Mother Teresa . . . the Dalai Lama— many have written about it as the key to happiness. But these wise leaders were not raising children. Does serving our own kids count toward the pursuit of happiness? Of course it does, but there is more to this pursuit. We know too many parents who devote their lives to their families and still feel unfulfilled. Maybe that's where the adventure comes in.

The Nuns and Cans of Parenting

Centuries ago, mapmakers used images of monsters to caution sailors against drifting into uncharted waters. In the pictures of the ocean, far beyond the well-worn trade routes, they drew these beasts as warnings: *Here be dragons.* Such threats kept most travelers within the sea lanes, but the bravest ventured beyond. They did not see portents. They saw adventure. They saw purpose. Likewise, as parents, we have tried to let our decisions be driven by possibility, not fear. We think it is possible to raise decent kids, be good to each other, and not give up hope that we can make some difference in the wider world.

Over the course of our marriage, we have learned to look for beacons to guide our journey. We like to call these the **Nuns and Cans of Parenting**. In boating terms, these are the numbered signs and buoys that line the channel into and out of the safety of the harbor. We think families would benefit from such channel markers, too. "This way to adventure." Or "Follow me, and I will guide you home."

The nature of Nuns and Cans involves both reaching out and reining in. Cans lead to exploration, purpose, unknown waters, and the perils of the open sea. Nuns bring refuge, time for reflection, and the security of a known harbor. As parents, we often feel pulled in separate directions. We strive to be full participants in the greater world and fully present at home. We struggle to find that balance between land and sea. When it comes to raising a family, especially when things go belly up, it is a good time to take stock of your Nuns and Cans and adjust course.

> **I** ADVENTURES ARE WORTH THE MISHAPS.

Parenting comes with fiascoes—the potty-training accident at the museum, the diaper blowout on the airplane, the stuffed unicorn left on the train. Sometimes it feels like you should never leave the house, never even attempt to navigate out to sea. But the opposite is true. Having children gives you a built-in excuse for misadventures. Embrace the mayhem, and plan some more.

 2 Love ruins plans.

Both of us are ambitious in our own ways. But our individual plans have sometimes been thrown off track because of love—for one another, for our children, and even for the wider world. Love does not always track a straight line or even a single course. But if you let love guide your way, you can never be lost, even when it leads you places you never intended to go.

3 Happiness is cheap.

And toys are expensive. It does not take nearly as much money as we used to think it did to be happy. Catching fish, building snowmen, drumming on pots and pans . . . kids are actually pretty good at cut-rate happiness. Sometimes, it is the smallest, most maneuverable boat that gets you where you need to go.

 4 Imbalance is balance.

When it comes to parenting, share the imbalance. *You cleaned up the barf yesterday, so I'll clean up the poop today. You did bedtime all week, so let me take care of it tonight.* Complete balance is an illusion, anyway. A sailboat underway is never perfectly upright. The fastest point of sail is a beam reach, the wind directly broadside, forcing the boat to lean over as it plows through the water. Like sailboats, the best marriages adjust to the prevailing winds.

5 Talk to strangers.

Gandhi—who was a parent—believed the surest path to happiness could be found in service to others. Embracing the world means opening our hearts. Although oceans may divide us, the world is indeed full of goodness and love, and we are better for accepting the kindness of strangers and for sharing what we have with those we've never met.

 You're not the boss of the applesauce.

Having children is humbling work. It is okay to loosen your grip and let other people take the lead. We have received parenting instruction from neighbors, schoolteachers, and friends at church. And, though we do not always like to admit it, our own children have taught us some of the most lasting lessons. We have learned patience, forgiveness, humility, and how adults can be pushed to the absolute brink of insanity and still gaze upon their children with love.

 Change your socks.

As a Navy pilot, Ken would tell this to his crew. It was his way of reminding them that in order to take care of their shipmates, they had to take care of themselves. The same is true for parents. This might mean sleeping late on Saturdays, volunteering at church, or escaping to a grown-ups-only trip to New York City. Figure out what you need in order to be able to be present for your children when it really matters.

 Every storm ends.

As a family, we've been buffeted here and there. Most of the time, we have navigated through those storms. But sometimes, you have to batten down the hatches. Lower the sails, forget about steering, and hunker down. Don't plan; just hold onto one another and pray. Eventually, even the fiercest storms blow over.

Never sail into a harbor you cannot sail out of.

Admiral Grace Hopper once said: "A ship in port is safe—but that is not what ships are for." It is one thing to take shelter during storms, but we are not meant to hide in port forever. It's a big ocean out there, with much to discover and more than a few sinking ships to save. To be part of the world, to be fully alive, to raise children who know the virtue of serving others, we must sometimes journey into rough seas.

What follows is a chronicle of where we went wrong and where we started to go right in our attempts to raise our children to be the people we hope they can be. We are not parenting experts. We are not even marriage experts. We have missed birthdays and Christmases to pursue the things we care about as individuals and as a family. We've even broken a promise or two. But we do our best to ensure our kids feel safe and loved and that they see their mom and dad leading meaningful lives. Whether it comes from teaching in a wilderness detention center or leading a relief mission in the Philippines, our hope is that however often we fall short as parents, we will still set an example our children would be proud to follow.

1. We Are Never Getting Married

I knew I would never marry Ken before I even met him.

It was the night before classes were to begin, and life was good. My freshman year in college had begun with such anxiety and heartache—meeting the strangers I'd be living with, seeing my parents sweaty and exhausted from the move-in as my eight-year-old brother cried that he was "never going to see me again." But this second year was old hat. Our dorm was air-conditioned. My roommates, Meg and Beena, were great people. I was jazzed about my classes. I had things under control.

I said hello to some friends down the hall, and they mentioned that their third roommate had never shown up. They were not concerned about his absence, however, and were already planning how to reconfigure the triple-sized room for two people. As I walked back to my own room, I remember wondering, *What kind of person doesn't show up for the first day of school?*

Ken later explained that he had been solo camping in the New Mexican wilderness and was late to school because he lost track of the days. This information did not improve his chances with me.

So how did the perfect-attendance girl who matched her T-shirts to her underwear meet the guy who drank expired milk and skipped the first day of school? The short answer is *I don't remember*. Ken claims we met when he and his roommate walked down the hall and knocked on my door. I have no memory of this encounter. To this day, when Ken protests, I remind him that "a lot of guys knocked on my door." He does not find this comforting.

I do remember the first time I noticed him. We lived in a service-themed residence hall, and all of us road-tripped to a North Carolina beach house one weekend to hang out and plan our charitable work for the semester. We played volleyball, nursed sunburns, and held the kind of meetings where giant Post-it notes were taped to the wall.

After dinner the first night, I saw a guy strumming a guitar near the ocean. He was fiddling with a Garth Brooks song and called over to a group of us, wondering if anyone knew the lyrics to "Friends in Low Places." The song had been the de facto graduation mantra for my high school senior class, so I said I would help him out. I sat down next to the stranger in the darkness. This was before cell phones and Google, back when the only things you knew were what you actually knew and what you could convincingly make up. It turned out that singing along with Garth Brooks on the radio was easier than singing with Ken. Also, *knowing of* a song and *knowing* a song are entirely different things. We got about two lines in before I discovered I did not know any other words except the chorus. But since I bring more confidence than skill to most situations, I just sang variations of the chorus again and again. It was a goofy first (or second) impression. But we both laughed and spent the next hour attempting other tunes we failed to finish. It was a night of beginnings.

We were a mismatch from the start, and not just musically. I volunteered at the local elementary school and sang in the concert choir. Ken played club soccer and crawled through the dorm ventilation shafts to play pranks on his neighbors. I audited extra classes and worked two jobs. Ken napped frequently and studied abroad as often as possible (the university finally cut him off after three semesters). But we were friends. Good friends. He was one of the first people I ever emailed, on a system called PINE that an engineering major told me about. I registered Ken for classes when he was studying in Australia. And when he was on campus, we ate dinner together, and we argued. Lots. About everything from the best Snapple flavors to health care reform.

But we did not date. Not for years, anyway. Not until the tornado. And the orphanage soccer game. And the bet over a lobster dinner.

During our junior year, I borrowed (without asking) and ruined (without mentioning) my roommate Beena's favorite sweater. She was peeved. Understandably. I asked what I could do to make it up to her.

"You can drive me to Kansas," she replied.

"I don't have a car, Beans," I reminded her.

"Get Ken to take me," she said.

"Why don't you ask him yourself?"

"I already did," she replied. "But he said he wouldn't do it . . . unless you come, too."

I lived outside of Cleveland, Ohio. Ken's people were in Montgomery, Alabama. Beena's west-of-the-Mississippi destination was not exactly on the way to either of our homes. But because of that ridiculous sweater, I agreed.

We planned to leave early on the Saturday after exams. Beena was packed and ready the night before. I awoke that morning to box up the last of my desk. Then Ken knocked on the door to see if I would help cut orange slices for his soccer game. I considered lecturing him about how a man's place was in the kitchen but changed my mind when he mentioned it was the last game of the season for the kids at Agape Corner, a children's boarding house where we had both volunteered that year.

The Agape kids were an awesome but rag-tag crew. Some had parents who couldn't handle them. Others had no parents at all. The house directors did their best to feed, clothe, and educate the children but sometimes fell short when it came to sports. Thus, there was tremendous excitement when Ken offered to coach a soccer team. Agape Corner hosted children of all ages, and, initially, the logistics of who would and would not be permitted to play became tricky. It was thought that a single team made exclusively of children from the school would make scheduling transportation and practice times easiest, but sorting through eligibility was daunting. Until Ken said, "Just sign 'em all up."

As a consequence, the Agape Strikers were assorted siblings and ne'er-do-wells, ranging in age from about seven to twelve. With a few almost-teenagers in the field, the team should have amassed an impressive winning record. But most of the kids had never played an organized sport before. Subpar coaching and faulty footwear made for tough progress. One child routinely wore slippers to practice. And despite Ken's emphasis on passing the ball, the Strikers competed in a tight scrum that only dispersed when the kids stopped to argue amongst themselves. "Hey, I had the ball!" "No fair!" "He kicked me!" "Jerk!"

That Saturday in early May found the team winless, heading into the final game of the season. Ken and I arrived for the warm-up, and the kids ran over, begging for oranges. "Sorry, you guys," I said. "These are for halftime." At the same instant, Ken opened the Tupperware container and said, "Here—who can catch an orange in his mouth?" If I had at all been imagining a future with this man, I might have reconsidered as I watched Ken and the kids warm up for a soccer game by beaning each other in the head with orange slices. Instead, I stepped back from the sideline as the ref blew the whistle for the start of play.

Our Strikers took the field like goldfish. They paid little heed to traditional starting positions and instead lollygagged from spot to spot. When the whistle blew and the scrum commenced, this game had all the trappings of previous bouts—missed kicks, frequent penalties, handballs, and dramatic injuries. The Strikers loved Band-Aids, ice packs, and attention. But the crumb-bum play was two-sided that day. And for once, the other team was as lousy as we were. The Agape Strikers fought the Durham Devils to a 1–1 draw.

That league did not do shoot-outs, so the score stood, and the kids celebrated their triumph with equal parts woots and squabbles. Our single goal had rolled free of the pack and wobbled past an unalert keeper late in the game, so there was some confusion over whose shot it had actually been. Before it came to blows, Ken suggested we all go to McDonald's to celebrate our victorious tie.

Two hours and fourteen Happy Meals later, we said good-bye to the Agape kiddos and headed back to campus.

Road-Trip Tetris

As we pulled up in front of the dorm, Ken said, "I just need to pack a few things."

We hopped out of the car and headed upstairs. When he opened the door to his room, I wondered if he had misunderstood our departure time. His desk was strewn with books and papers, scrunched-up napkins, and takeout containers. There were still sheets on his bed, posters on the walls, and clothes on the floor in his closet. And something was definitely rotting in a bag next to the chair in the corner. In short, his room looked exactly as it had all year long. We were supposed to leave for Kansas right now, and Ken had not packed anything yet.

"Should I tell Beena we're going to leave tomorrow instead?" I asked.

"Nah, I'm good. Give me, like, ten minutes," he replied. "Why don't you guys bring your stuff down to the car?"

He tossed me the keys, and I went to find my roommate. We brought our boxes, bags, mixtapes, and snacks down to Ken's beat-up Pathfinder. We were still strategizing suitcases and seating arrangements when Ken appeared with two large black trash bags.

"These can go in," he said. "But I need to make one more trip."

Beena and I began the life-size game of Tetris that constitutes any good car-packing job, with the rectangular suitcases at the base of the cargo area and odd-shaped items on top. We had filled the space perfectly when Ken returned with three more trash bags and a lamp.

"We're gonna need a bigger boat," I said.

"Either that or the code to Nathan's storage unit," Ken said. He called one of his roommates, Nathan, who had already hit the road, and asked for his super-secret storage unit password, which, if I'm not mistaken, turned out to be "1-2-3-4." We eased ourselves into the stuffed truck. I sat on a milk crate in the back seat, covered in trash bags and holding the ugly wooden lamp in my lap. When we arrived at the storage unit and rolled up the metal door, we realized other hop-ons had beaten us to the punch. The unit was already stuffed to the gills with couches, duffel bags, and other people's ugly lamps. It looked like a larger version of Ken's truck.

"I don't think your junk is gonna fit," I said.

"Are you kidding?" Ken replied. "There's still tons of room in here." Whereas I had seen the cubicle as half-full, Ken saw it as half-empty. He stepped on the first couch and then onto the second that was jauntily stacked on top of it, ducked under the overhanging door, and tossed the first of his bags up and over the piles of crap that would furnish our classmates' rooms in the fall. Ken stuffed the remaining bags inside, and the three of us coerced the door shut.

"Who's hungry?" Ken asked.

"Hungry?" I replied.

"Yeah," said Beena, "shouldn't we try to get through the mountains before dark?"

"We are about to traverse half of Appalachia," Ken observed. "Not exactly the easiest place to find late-night food. And with a drive this long, there's no way we can avoid the darkness. Might as well start the long haul on a full stomach." We ended up at a chicken-and-biscuits place for our last supper.

Just after seven thirty, twelve short hours after our—well, what turned out to be Beena's and my—target departure time, we headed for the interstate. Thus began the meandering and circuitous route to each of our homes. With the three destinations of Cleveland, Kansas City, and Montgomery, the "quickest route," if it could be called that, would have been a counterclockwise path—northwest out of North Carolina to Ohio, southwest to Kansas, and then southeast back to Alabama. But Ken insisted that I help him get Beena home, so we skipped Ohio and headed to Kansas first.

Beena did not yet know how to handle a stick-shift car, so Ken and I took turns driving through the night. Around one thirty in the morning, somewhere in Tennessee, Beena and I saw lights in the distance. It looked like pyrotechnics at a rock concert. As we got closer, we realized it was a lightning storm, one of the largest I had ever seen. The wind kicked up, shaking the car, and before I knew it, I was driving through a torrential downpour with near-zero visibility. I flicked on my hazard lights, gripped the steering wheel, and asked Beena to help me see the painted highway lines. We flipped through radio stations until we heard one issue an emergency weather warning. I had only ever heard practice beeps before. This was the real thing. The broadcast that followed alerted listeners in Sumner County, Tennessee, to take shelter from a tornado.

"What county are we in?" I asked Beena.

Our cheap gas-station map of the southeastern United States was not broken into counties. For all we knew, we were driving right into the path of a tornado. I panicked. Should we pull off? Hide under a bridge? Were we safe in the car, or did we need to find shelter somewhere? Ken, who suffered from motion sickness when he sat in the backseat, had slept through the entirety of the storm. Until now. He reached his hand forward to my shoulder and rubbed it gently, saying, "Everything is going to be okay." Looking back, I realize that Ken did not have any empirical data to support this statement. He did not know which county we were in or whether we were driving into the

I believed him. He steadied me. Because he had said so, I knew we would be safe.

 Every Storm Ends

maw of a great storm. But I believed him. He steadied me. Because he had said so, I knew we would be safe. Every storm ends.

We found an exit and pulled off to watch the rest of the tempest through the windows of a Waffle House. Ken drove the next shift, and now it was my turn to drowse in the tiny backseat. At some point in the darkness, he also grew too tired to drive, and I awoke around seven thirty the next morning, with a sore neck and pins and needles in my feet, to discover that all three of us had fallen asleep in the parking lot of a rest area somewhere near the Missouri border.

We splashed cold water on our faces, Beena and I brushed our teeth, and we drove the bright, flat route to Kansas unmolested any further by weather. We feasted on Beena's mother's homemade pot stickers that night. Not realizing they were only the appetizer, Ken ate seventeen of them, only to open his eyes wide in confusion when Beena's mom brought out the chicken, pork, vegetables, and fried rice. You had to hand it to him—days were never dull when Ken was around. I slept on a mattress on Beena's floor that night with a full belly and a full heart. Ken and I set out for Ohio the following morning.

We could have made it in one day, but there were detours, hiccups, and, as usual, adventures that turned into mishaps and stretched one day into three. A hike in Kentucky turned into a camping trip. After two days of roughing it without a proper tent, when I complained that I did not wish to arrive home looking like a hobo, Ken found me a truck stop where I paid for a hot shower and changed into clean clothes. I was not accustomed to spur-of-the-moment bivouacking or bathing in Texacos. I was ready to get home. But this ridiculous boy had gotten under my skin.

We played a game during the drive that involved sharing highs and lows from each of our twelve years of elementary and high school. My low was losing the Arbor Day poster contest in the third grade. And my second-grade high was being runner up in the read-a-thon and winning a watch.

"Were you always competitive as a child?" Ken asked me.

"No," I said. "As long as I won."

When it was Ken's turn to share a high point, he paused. I sensed he was holding back. "Canoeing with my dad," he said finally. It was years later before I learned that the two of them had canoed in Scotland. Across Loch Ness. So much for impressing him with my read-a-thon watch.

Ken dropped me off in Ohio, spent the night on a foldout couch in our living room, and shoved off for Alabama the next day. Neither of us declared anything formal, but we both knew something had changed. Depending on the traffic around Atlanta, the drive from Duke University to Montgomery, Alabama should take about half a day. By adding in Kansas City and Cleveland, Ken's journey from school to home took 118 hours.

When I called Beena to tell her about the trip, she said, "Yes . . . I knew it!"

"What are you talking about?" I asked.

"I bet Ken a lobster dinner that the two of you would start dating." I started to protest that nothing had happened, that we weren't "dating," but I could not even convince myself. She had traded her sweater for a lobster dinner. And I had myself a boyfriend.

But even when we returned to school in the fall, I knew this was a short-term thing. We had lots of fun—dances and dinners, movies, more arguments, and a couple of moonlit walks—but I always knew this wasn't for keeps. Even over graduation weekend, I told my mom and grandma that dating Ken had "been fun, but I had no intention of following that boy all around the country." Sure, I liked him, but he was joining the Navy, and I would not hitch my wagon to that particular boat.

Except when I went home to Ohio after graduation, I missed him.

I missed his good humor, his tenderness, his nerve. I missed the way he talked about honor and doing something bigger than himself. I understood service—I was awaiting word from an inner-city teaching job in Chicago. But Ken spoke of purpose in ways I had never heard someone our age say before. In spite of all the ideas I had about my future, I could feel myself falling for him. Whatever plans I had were soon going to be ruined. Love has a way of doing that.

The Girl Who Peed on Me

The summer after graduation, instead of packing for Chicago, I found myself interviewing for teaching positions down south. Ken was heading to pilot training in Pensacola. Maybe I would find a job in Florida, too. I wanted to teach tough kids. Did it really matter where I found them?

I accepted an offer from a wilderness rehabilitation program for troubled teens. Eckerd Youth Alternatives had over eight hundred acres of pine forests, hiking trails, and cockroaches. Counselors worked on site five days a week, twenty-four hours a day, living side by side with the young people they served. My family thought I was nuts for even considering it. I thought it sounded perfect. After years of papers and classes and tests and school, I was ready for real work. These kids needed stability, patience, someone to believe in them and listen. I signed a two-year contract, leased my first car, and drove away in August for a new adventure.

Though I did end up in the same state as Ken, we were nearly five hundred miles apart. As to how I did not realize that, I will chalk up to youth. Or love. Or maybe just not looking more carefully at the scale on my Florida road atlas—where one inch equaled 50 miles. Ken and I lived ten inches apart, but one of us made the nearly eight-hour drive every week or two.

My job was . . . challenging. It was hot. Florida hot. A-hundred-degrees-in-the-shade kind of hot. And humid. It was not unusual to

In spite of all the ideas I had about my future, I could feel myself falling for him.

2 Love Ruins Plans

sweat through our clean clothes within minutes of stepping out of the shower house. The place was teeming with wildlife. For the first few months, I had trouble sleeping because of the constant noise of deer, raccoons, and armadillos walking, shuffling, and burrowing beside my sleeping tent. I spent a few weeks battling a family of mice who insisted on sharing my cot. Every night, I would chase them out, and each morning, I would find them back again. And the mosquitos—at any given time, I had a couple dozen bites on my arms, legs, and face. I got my first tick bite in Florida. And my first (and second) case of head lice. But these physical trials were nothing compared with the emotional challenges I encountered.

I was a teacher and counselor at a therapeutic residential wilderness treatment center for girls. Which is code for "I lived in the woods with juvenile delinquents." On good days, we canoed, hiked, chopped down trees, and built our own shelters. We cooked over open fires and ate under blue skies. And therapy happened everywhere. On bad days, I broke up fistfights and restrained kids, sat up late with a teenager threatening suicide, and wondered whether I was making any difference at all. Some of the kids were anxious and depressed; many had substance abuse issues; a few were felons. Some of the girls had a teardrop or two tattooed beneath their eyes. It was rumored that meant they had killed somebody. These young people were mouthy and emotional and hormonal and pissed off, and yet, of all the children I have ever taught, they are the ones whose names and faces stick with me the most.

There was Ellen*, who was academically off the charts but also communicated daily with chipmunks. She had been sent to camp for assaulting her mother. There was Katrina, who hid candy in bathrooms but was also a gifted artist. Her parents had been killed in a car accident. She had bounced from one foster family to another and would never be adopted. One of my toughest kids was also one of my youngest. Ten-year-old

---

*To protect their privacy, I am not using the real names of any of the girls from camp.

Angela was angry, violent, and broken. Her mother was a drug addict, her father was in prison, and her adopted family had found her impossible to control. When she threw tantrums that risked harming herself or others, I was required to put her in a therapeutic restraining hold. I would wrap my arms around her until she calmed down. I had been trained in this maneuver. After one restraint, sometimes two, most children realized I was there to help them, to shield them, that I would not let them hurt themselves or be hurt by anyone else. But Angela was not like most other children. She used these confrontations as yet another way to lash out at her caregivers. She peed on me almost every time. These days, as a mom, I am used to bodily fluids—pee, poop, barf—I have contended with all of them before breakfast. But back then, as a twenty-three-year-old, this was my first experience with the many ways that young people can find to push your buttons. People sometimes marvel at my patience or my ability to stay calm when my own kids misbehave. I credit Angela for some of my first practice with the challenges of motherhood.

But of all the faces that I remember from camp, Tonya's is the one I have never been able to shake.

Tonya was angry. At her parents. At the system. At some guy up in Tallahassee who told her he loved her but who never once wrote to see if she was okay. And since mine was the face she saw every day, she was also pissed at me.

In the heat of a Florida day, when chores were finished and spirits were high, we retreated to our tents for the daily afternoon siesta. The girls wrote letters, rearranged their foot lockers, and daydreamed about being somewhere else. Tonya always slept. At the end of an hour or so, I gave the kids a five-minute cleanup time, and they put away their things and came out.

Except Tonya. There was no waking that kid up. I always figured she was faking it. Nobody could sleep that deeply.

We would cajole and yell and jiggle her shoulder and shake the cot under her mosquito net.

And she would not move.

It was like the darkness behind her eyes was better than anything we could offer her out in the light.

It was like she wanted to die.

There were two kinds of kids at camp: those sent by their families and those sentenced by a judge. The first group stayed as long as their parents' insurance or budget or patience would allow. Often, once a child made a little progress, Mom or Dad would pull her from the program. I remember being angry at those parents. Didn't they realize that Keisha, Tracey, and Gabriela needed more time? The girls had not yet found the inner strength to say no to bad "friends" and yes to the future. Didn't those parents see the risk of yanking their kids out at the very moment when they were finally seeing some success?

Now that I am a mom, I look back on those families and can hardly bear thinking about their heartache, about the fact that they were so desperate to save their daughters that they sent them away to live at a residential treatment facility in the middle of nowhere. All they wanted was for their girls to be safe. I have spoken to plenty of camp kids in the years since. They are now grown women, many of whom credit the time at that treatment facility with saving their lives. But I have not spoken to many parents. I can only imagine that the entire experience is one they would rather forget.

Tonya had not been placed at camp by her parents. She had been sent there by a judge. Usually, court-appointed campers were repeat offenders. They started with shoplifting, then truancy, maybe gang activity or drugs. Often breaking and entering or vandalism landed them in the same court again and again. The judge, running out of options and tired of seeing them in and out of a traditional detention center, would offer one last chance: Complete the wilderness program, kiddo. Save yourself.

Tonya was one of those kids. If she wanted out of camp, she was going to have to work on her goals. Or run away. Because no one would pick her up early. No one was coming for her.

In the first days of her stay, Tonya kept to herself. She walked where we asked her to walk, ate when we asked her to eat, and swept when we gave her a broom. But when the first home visit roster came out and her name was not listed, it was as though she realized the enormity of the prison she was in. She would not put up with it anymore. While the other girls in our group prepared to go home for a long weekend, to practice their goals in their family environment, Tonya would stay at camp with a handful of other girls. And me.

It was like all the strength went out of Tonya after that. When we asked her to take her laundry up the trail, she crumpled to the ground. She preyed upon other girls' fears and made it her goal to make people feel worse instead of better. In therapy like this, everything happens together. We ate as a group, cleaned as a group, and moved from place to place as a group. But Tonya did everything in her power to sabotage any possibility of success. If she could not go home, she was going to ruin everyone else's chances, too.

Tonya's first six months at camp were brutal. She plotted to run away to Miami with one of our other tough group members. She picked on the most vulnerable kids, the ones who wore anxiety and low self-esteem on their sleeves. She took a swing at me when I confronted her about the bullying. We ended up, both of us, caught in a ten-minute restraint in the dirt. She called me more names than I have ever been called since.

My co-counselor and I decided Tonya needed a project. She needed to see something grow or last or flourish as a result of the work of her two hands. While the rest of the group researched and plotted a course for our next canoeing trip, Tonya and I worked on a lean-to for organizing tools in our campsite. We drew up the plans, sawed down the trees, skinned off the bark, used post-hole diggers to bore deep into the root- and clay-riddled soil, and slowly cut, notched, and hammered our structure into place. Over the course of these hours and days, we talked. About little things at first: our favorite ice cream and how much we missed air conditioning. But then we moved onto other things. Tonya told me that she wrote poetry, that she liked to cook, and that she had loved her nephew like a brother. When he died on the streets, Tonya figured she was next. I came to understand how anger could mask sadness in a child's heart. Here was a thirteen-year-old kid who had seen more death and disappointment than I could dream of. She had sought shelter from her destructive family in the arms of a powerful street gang, and when their crimes became too much to handle, she had no place else to turn.

I would love to say that because we built a tool shed together, Tonya was set on the road to recovery. But, of course, that is not how it works. Her path was rocky and steep. And a lot of awful days followed the good ones. But we kept her busy, kept offering new challenges and experiences. We canoed the Suwanee River, swam in its cold springs, and camped along its muddy banks. We spent two weeks on a ropes course using physical challenges to confront our issues of control, fear, and trust. We even participated in an exchange program where we got to spend part of the winter in another camp in Vermont. It was on this trip, in the middle of yet another of Tonya's blowouts, that I asked her, "Who are you so angry at?" Without hesitation, she launched into a litany of everybody who had ever let her down. Then she sat down in the snow and started to cry.

In the months that we had known Tonya, we had heard her cuss, fart, burp, complain, and shout. But we had never seen her weep. Nobody quite knew what to do. So we just sat there in the growing darkness and told her we were there for her. I watched these kids—who had been thrown out of their homes, who had done and said terrible things to one another and to most of the people they loved—offer this hardened gang member their support. That lesson has stayed with me. We cannot undo all the damage we have wrought. Our mistakes leave scars. But when it comes to children, there is no hand I cannot hold. Most of those kids were in camp because the adults in their lives let them down. Adults had not provided them with enough consistency, with enough purpose, adventure, or love to navigate the difficulties of their childhood. That night with Tonya, I learned that sometimes, all it takes to be worthy of a child's love is to stand by them.

It took her almost a year and a half, but Tonya eventually graduated from our program. She learned to channel her sadness and strength into leadership, into writing, into goal-setting and self-care. She brought other girls into our group and showed them how to open up and trust. We spent twenty-eight days one November hiking, camping, and canoeing the Florida backcountry. It was so cold most nights that we ate dinner around four thirty, just as it was getting dark, and got into our tents by a quarter after six to try to get warm. Many kids who ended up at camp had been forced to grow up too fast. They had been stripped of their childhoods. So I did what I could to make up for lost time. I read them Dr. Seuss bedtime stories and *Goodnight Moon*, and we worked our way up to tween novels and even an abridged version of *Pride and Prejudice*. My co-counselors and I sang them lullabies and taught them games. We washed their feet around our campfire. I would go on to teach for a dozen years in classrooms all over the country, but I got my foundation, my belief in the goodness of every child, hiking the dusty trails of rural Florida with teenagers who had allowed themselves to be convinced that they were no good.

When my two years were up, I was conflicted. I had worked 120-hour weeks, eating, sleeping, and living at my job. It was grueling work, but I loved it. And I was good at it. Part of me wanted to stay. But part of me knew I was shredded. My hair was falling out. I dreamed about the kids during my time off. I had not been to the dentist in a year and a half. And I had someone else who had been waiting, supporting me while I supported these kids. In the end, I decided to leave.

On my last day at camp, all of the counselors and kids threw me a fake wedding in the capture-the-flag field, complete with costumes, songs, and a sermon from one of my most ridiculously wonderful kids. Ken even made a surprise entrance, having driven all night to be there. In one final bizarre and loving gesture, the kids framed my bathing suit and hung it—like a retired sports jersey—above the community bathroom.

Five weeks later, I got married for real. I guess after twenty-four months with juvenile delinquents, a lifetime with Ken didn't seem so bad.

2: WE ARE NEVER HAVING CHILDREN

I always knew I was going to marry this girl. She could pretend all she wanted, but deep down, she realized I was the only guy who could handle her kind of crazy. The job she took at the juvenile offender camp? Her whole family was baffled by it. But I understood. It may not have made dating her any easier, but it did make me realize how much I loved her. We saw the world the same way and often talked about how we could do good things together while still leading exciting lives.

For me, that search for purpose and adventure led me to join the Navy. For Annmarie, that meant building shelters in the woods with a bunch of unpredictable teenagers. For both of us, our jobs were enough. When we daydreamed about a life together, it did not involve having children of our own. After completing flight school, I would deploy overseas six months of every year. That would be hard enough on our relationship. There was no need to throw kids into that mix. Besides, Annmarie felt like she already had kids. She loved those girls at camp as though they were her own. She could not envision her heart ever needing more.

She made $233 a week at camp. I made a bit more as a newly minted naval officer, but I spent a good chunk of that money driving back and forth to see her. Florida is a big state, and it has that weird elbow around the Gulf of Mexico. With Annmarie at the thumb (near Tampa) and me at the armpit (lovely Pensacola), the drive between us was basically a half day's commitment and $35 in gas.

Sometimes, we'd split the difference. One weekend, we met in the parking lot of a diner off Highway 98. They did not accept credit cards, and when we pooled our spare change, we had exactly $6.75. Annmarie wanted the mozzarella sticks. But since fried cheese is gross, and since most of the change piled on the table was mine, I ordered four crab claws and a slice of key lime pie.

I asked for lemons and sugar (free) and made some killer lemonade right in front of her. She claims this had nothing to do with her falling for me, but that woman loved her lemonade.

"You gotta trust me here," I said. I asked for lemons and sugar (free) and made some killer lemonade right in front of her. She claims this had nothing to do with her falling for me, but that woman loved her lemonade. We spent six months like this—rendezvousing at Waffle Houses and roadside diners, doing whatever it took to see each other. It was becoming apparent (to me at least) that love alone wasn't going to keep us together. We needed to *be* together. Being a fix-it kind of guy, I came up with a solution.

3 | HAPPINESS IS CHEAP

I decided to propose. I would ask, she would say yes (with a single tear running down her cheek), then she would quit her job and I could stop spending entire weekends driving to see her and making hobo lemonade. As luck would have it, I got a helpful assist from my fiancée-to-be.

Barely a week after I bought the ring, Annmarie planned a getaway for the two of us to Dog Island. The name is unfair. The island is a sparse but beautiful patch of sand off the Gulf Coast, windswept and barren but for a few beach cottages. Also, the only way to get there is by ferry. Arranging our rendezvous, Annmarie was emphatic. "You HAVE to be there by 3:00 p.m. to catch the boat," she said over the phone.

I left the Naval Air Station early, changed out of my flight suit in the car, and arrived at the ferry dock with time to spare. I did not have my proposal totally planned, but figured I would know when the right moment presented itself. I wanted the ring with me just in case, so I took it out of its velvet box, slipped it into a zip-lock bag, and slid it into my pocket. Every few minutes, I reached down to make sure it was still there.

Three o'clock came and went, along with the ferry that was meant to spirit us to our weekend getaway. Annmarie was nowhere to be found. I knew better than to worry. Being late to things was part of her crazy. Her "charm," she would say. I gritted my teeth, preparing a speech about the importance of reliability. But every time I started to get mad, I felt the ring in my pocket. I was one of the few people she could afford to let down. With the stresses of her job, all those kids depending on her, I was the last person who had any right to be demanding.

The day wore on. Eventually, her beat-up Honda pulled up to the dock. You know you love someone when your anger melts away upon seeing her.

"Well," I asked, "what's our backup plan?"

"I see a lot of boats," she said. "I'll just ask one of them to take us."

That was her solution. No apology. No admission. Not even the slightest awareness that the predicament we found ourselves in was entirely one person's fault. I nearly pointed all of this out, except that Annmarie was already working on a boat captain in the neighboring slip. He was clearly done for the day, lugging a cooler onto the dock.

"I'd be more than happy to," he said.

That is, more than happy to fire up the engine, load up two strangers, head back out to sea, and take us someplace he did not need to go. Things always seem to go like this for Annmarie. Whenever our plans seem irrecoverably ruined, she manages to turn those mishaps into yet another adventure.

I felt the ring in my pocket one last time, grabbed my bag from the car, and hopped aboard. We arrived late, settled into our cottage after finding the key under the mat, and headed out for a stroll on the beach.

Ever since that first beach night back in college, we had been inching closer to this moment. It was like something out of a movie, lapping waves as the soundtrack, setting sun as the stage lighting. I slid the ring from my pocket and took a knee.

It did not go as I had imagined.

"What are you doing?" Annmarie asked.

"Umm . . ." I said. "Will you, y'know, marry me?"

"Now?" she asked. "You're asking me this *now*?"

I had prepared for an assortment of responses—joy, tears, speechlessness. Cross-examination was not one of them. I stammered something about how awesome she was. When she still had not responded, I gestured toward the ring. "I got you a ring," I said, in case she had been confused about the intended recipient of the gemstone I clutched in my now very sweaty hands.

Annmarie did not act like the girls in the movies. She did not swoon at the sight of a diamond. Instead, in her own colorful way, she explained that my "timing was horrible," that she had "life plans" and "a commitment to these camp kids," and, most of all, that "this was MY weekend getaway." She had planned the whole trip, and the last time she checked, it most certainly "did not include a marriage proposal."

"Did it include missing the ferry?" I asked. I can see now that this was probably a mistake. But by that point, I was not at my best. My knee had lost all feeling, and my head was racing. I sat down in the sand.

Annmarie sat down next to me. "At least let me see it," she said. I handed her the ring, half wondering if she would throw it into the sea.

Perhaps it was because the wind had picked up and we were getting cold. Or maybe because we were stuck on an island together for the next twenty-four hours. Whatever the reason, in the end, I got my answer: "I guess so, but not for another year or two, at least."

Though my proposal had gone badly off the rails, once that ring was finally out of my pocket and on her finger, deep down, I had no doubts. One way or another, whether Annmarie realized it or not, we were going to spend the rest of our lives together.

At this point in the story, sometimes folks ask me, "What happened next?" Did she quit her job and start planning our dream wedding? No. Did she work at that godforsaken (but still awesome) camp for another year and a half? Yes. Did she keep the engagement ring (two months of salary!) in a change purse in her unlocked cubby at work? Of course she did.

For another eighteen months, we kept up our ridiculous ritual, driving eight hours each way to see each other. She kept her promise to serve that camp for two years, and on her last day, the kids staged us a fake wedding—with a dress from Goodwill, a Betty Crocker cake, and a groom smuggled into an all-girls facility after another all-night sprint across half the state of Florida.

CAPTURED BY PIRATES ON OUR HONEYMOON

Eventually, the real wedding happened on a perfect October day in Ohio. I was in my Navy mess dress, with newly pinned aviator wings. Not that anyone noticed, because all eyes were on the bride. We tied the knot and pulled away from the church in a horse-drawn carriage driven by my mom (a little weird, but in a romantic kind of way). The honeymoon, however, would have to wait. I was on a tight timeline to finish pilot training and had only twenty-four hours of leave remaining before I needed to return to my Navy base.

We scheduled our departure for the next morning in time to get back to Jacksonville before my next training sortie.

Guess what?

We missed the plane.

Guess whose fault?

Not saying.

Within twenty minutes, though, Annmarie had sweet-talked her way past an AirTran ticket agent and gotten us two seats on the next flight for twenty-five dollars each. My girl.

We made it home in time, and the following weekend, we drove down to Cape Canaveral National Seashore for our honeymoon. We canoed through the marshlands, fished, played Scrabble by firelight, and one magical afternoon watched a space shuttle carrying John Glenn rocket into space. It was a camping trip for the books.

Even though Annmarie never complained, I worried I was letting my new bride down. She had given up camp and felt like she had abandoned her kids, all to be with me. Annmarie had sacrificed part of what made her her. And what had I offered in return? A two-day honeymoon—camping.

Plus, my assignment to Jacksonville was temporary. For six months, we lived in a hotel room on the airbase. Most mornings, I woke at four o'clock to fly. Annmarie was a teacher but did not want to accept a year-long position, since I would be reassigned to another squadron in the spring. She took her commitment to kids seriously. So she kept busy, teaching instead as a high school substitute: not exactly glamorous work. She came home with plenty of wacky stories—about the kid who crawled under her desk and called her dirty names or the ones who asked to use the bathroom and never came back. She spent most of one day assigned to "parking lot duty." But even the most ill-organized schools eventually realized the talent they were wasting. Two different high schools asked her to apply for full-time positions. But we would be leaving Jacksonville soon. She did not want to accept a job knowing she would have to leave it when the time came for my reassignment. So she stayed in her holding pattern while I finished flight school. I consoled myself with the fact that once I was through, there would be time for the teaching career—and the honeymoon—she deserved.

In the spring, I got my orders to Washington State. Annmarie set about applying for jobs. And in my spare time, I began planning our actual honeymoon. The key, like any military tactician will tell you, was maintaining the element of surprise.

The plan looked great on paper—Annmarie and I, alone together in a sailboat just big enough for the two of us, island-hopping across the Ionian Sea around Greece. A week before we were to leave, she still had no idea where we were headed.

"Will it be warm?" she asked.

"Umm . . . yeah," I said.

"Will I need a swimsuit?" she asked.

"No," I said, because, you know, I didn't want to ruin the surprise.

So we flew to Athens, rented a car, and headed north along the Greek coastline.

"Is this the surprise?" she asked.

"Not yet," I said.

As we drove past the tiny fishing villages, Annmarie began to understand what was happening to her.

"Tell me the TRUTH," she said. "Are we going sailing? You promised me we were NOT going sailing on our HONEYMOON."

"I did?" I answered.

Looking back, it is a good thing I kept that crucial fact from her, or I never would have gotten her on that boat. As it happened, she had no choice. She was stuck with me in a Greek fishing village with a one-way rental car and her honeymoon sloop right there. In such a situation, there is not much to do but head for open water with the man you now hate.

But first, we had to meet the owner, an expat Englishman who seemed to be a permanent fixture at the dockside tavern, cigarette in hand and half-empty ouzo bottle within easy reach. I assumed I would have to pass a seamanship test or at least demonstrate some basic knowledge of sailing. Like which part of the boat was the front.

None of that happened. He tossed me the keys and said, "Good luck, mate." Then he added, "Whatever happens, just do NOT give up the pink paper."

"Why not?" I asked.

"Because whoever has that paper," he said, jabbing his cigarette toward the dock, "owns the boat."

I nodded, dumbly trying to imagine a scenario in which I might be asked to give away his vessel.

We spent the rest of that first afternoon shopping for sundries and a swimsuit. "How do you say 'size ten' in Greek?" Annmarie grumbled after a saleslady handed her a bikini fit for a four-year-old. After purchasing a bottle of aloe that turned out to be dish detergent, we returned to our boat. We spent the night dockside, then headed out at dawn. I had sailed many times with my family, sleeping, eating, and playing on crafts not much bigger than this one. But Annmarie had not. In fact, the one time we had been sailing together, she complained that the vessel was "too tippy" and made me take her back to the dock. I had conveniently forgotten that until just now. Also, the more I thought about it, my parents had actually done most of the sailing while I, routinely seasick, slept below. Annmarie and I were quite a pair then, the seasick captain and his cranky first mate.

Luckily, Annmarie's anger cooled. It was kind of romantic, she admitted, sailing around Greece on our honeymoon. She got the hang of running the rigging, and—when I was not asleep or yacking over the gunnel—I kept our course. It seemed like a metaphor for the life we were embarking on. There would be rocky patches, even storms, but we would overcome them. Together, we would find our way.

Two days into the trip, after lunch in a rocky cove, we pulled up anchor and motored out to open water to hoist the sails. Suddenly, the engine died. We had to make a choice: we could sail back into the cove and anchor again or continue out to sea. With hills all around, the wind was unpredictable. We knew we could maneuver back into the cove, but thought we might have difficulty getting out again. The nearest harbor was roughly an hour away. If our engine needed work, it made sense to head there. So we hoisted the sails. The wind was steady, and we made good time, but the approach to the harbor was narrow and rocky. We circled once but could not safely pull in under sail power alone. I jumped on the radio to see whether anyone who spoke a little English could tow us the rest of the way in.

Not ten minutes after I made the call, a boat full of Greeks pulled up. It was like they had been waiting for us.

One of them had a tiny video camera and filmed the whole thing. They pulled alongside us, and I threw them a rope, which they immediately threw back. It seemed odd, but I thought nothing of it as they heaved over their own line. I grabbed it and tied off. The man with the camera waved. I gave him a thumbs up sign in return.

When we pulled up to the dock, our Greek rescuers lived up to their countrymen's reputation for friendliness. We offered them money and a bottle of wine, but they graciously declined. They helped us tie our boat to the dock and motored across the harbor.

"Wow, they were really great," Annmarie said. She opened a jar of olives, and I looked below for a corkscrew for the wine. Neither of us saw the uniformed man saunter down the dock.

"Hello. Can I help you?" I heard Annmarie say as the boat rocked side to side. I headed above deck to see that the uniformed man had helped himself aboard. Normally, one does not board another's boat without asking permission.

"Pink paper," he said, holding out his hand.

"Sorry?" I said.

"I will have pink paper," he said.

I started to protest. "Actually, I can't give you that paper. Sorry, but the owner was very clear about—"

"I will have pink paper," he said again.

"It's just that that's the title to the boat. If we could just give the owner a quick call . . ."

"The pink paper . . . please." He smiled and held out his hand, but the look in his eyes told both of us that his "please" was a courtesy. He was not asking.

Annmarie put her hand on my arm. "Babe, I think this gentleman would like the pink paper. Why don't you see if you can find it?"

I shook my head, ducked into the cabin, and emerged moments later with the paper. So much for me holding our course.

Here's what had happened. When I accepted the tow line from their tug, I had granted them legal salvage rights to a boat adrift. And it was all on tape. The cop, we learned later, was the tug driver's brother, and this was a racket he had run many times before. After we gave him the pink paper, he escorted us up the hill to the village jail. Apparently, even without an engine, we were a flight risk. They did not want us to leave with what was now their boat. We spent the afternoon watching *Baywatch* reruns with far more police than could possibly have been required for such a tiny village. They asked about life in America and whether we had ever met Pamela Anderson. When we admitted we had not, they fell mostly silent. Ms. Anderson is, in fact, Canadian. But that was a detail I spared our hosts.

Later in the day, our boat's former owner arrived to bail us out. He had a five-gallon gas can in one hand, and with the other, he was smoking a cigarette. In exchange for a large wad of cash, they gave him back the pink paper.

He was surprisingly zen about the whole episode.

"Price of business," he said. Turns out, the engine was fine. It was just out of gas, and the gauge was stuck at three-quarters full, a fact he knew but had forgotten to mention.

The rest of our honeymoon was only slightly less adventurous. We finished our ten days on the boat, hopping lazily from island to island. We left Greece, capped off our trip with a whirlwind tour of Israel, then headed back stateside to pack up for my new assignment.

Here's the thing: when my wife and I reminisce about big moments together, these adventurous mishaps are the ones that stand out. We made some wonderful memories on our honeymoon—climbing Masada in Israel, exploring the Parthenon in Athens—but the story that stands out, the one we tell again and again, is of being captured by a friendly band of Greek pirates outside of a fishing village on the Ionian Sea.

The story that stands out, the one we tell again and again, is of being captured by a friendly band of Greek pirates outside of a fishing village on the Ionian Sea.

1 | ADVENTURES ARE
WORTH THE MISHAPS

4:33 A.M.

I did finish flight school. And Annmarie and I did survive our first six months of married life cramped in a hotel room. Although, to be fair, she did cause the entire building to be evacuated when she set off the fire alarm trying to bake me a birthday cake in the microwave. Regardless, I managed to graduate as the top Navy pilot from my training class, and I chose to fly the ugliest airframe in the US military. The EP-3 is slow and boring with four smoking prop engines like some bomber from World War II. But it is packed to the gills with sophisticated surveillance equipment and is tasked with some of our nation's most critical reconnaissance missions.

I was stationed on a Navy base on Whidbey Island, Washington. As happy as we were about this new adventure together, we were fully aware that my job would take me away for months on end, often with little notice. Annmarie did not sit back and mope. She found a teaching gig near Seattle and poured herself into it. There was only one problem: her school was two hours from my base on the island. Most of the time, it did not matter. Since I was deployed for half the year, Annmarie rented a tiny room in a house close to where she worked. It got her commute down to eleven minutes. Early on, Annmarie made the mistake of telling her mother about our separate residences. "Don't tell your grandma," she made Annmarie promise. Our adventures sometimes look like mistakes to other people.

When I was home, we did our best to stay in the same place, our house on Whidbey Island or her rented room in Seattle, as often as possible. As the crow flies, they were not far apart. So if we had been birds, the commute would have been manageable. But as mortals doomed to drive, one of us had to make the long looping journey north to Deception Pass, over Swinomish Channel—with a quick stop at the coffee hut in the gas station parking lot and then sixty-seven miles of interstate back south. It was like a miniature version of the Florida drive we had endured while Annmarie was at camp. But because Seattle traffic was all rain and bridges and fog and black ice, for Annmarie to make her 7:30 a.m. school bell, that meant leaving Whidbey Island at 4:30 in the morning.

For the most part, we made it work. Sometimes, I stayed with her in Seattle. But we liked our house on Whidbey Island better than her rented room, so more often than not, Annmarie was the one making the drive. I tried not to worry too much or feel too guilty about her epic commute. Except for once, when she called me after getting to school.

"It was real," she said.

"What?"

"The mountain lion," she said.

"What mountain lion?" I said. "What are you talking about?"

I thought she was kidding, but Annmarie was serious. She insisted, in her lovably irrational way, that a full-grown mountain lion had been sleeping in the middle of the road as she had pulled out of our driveway three hours earlier.

"Okaaay," I said. I was fairly certain that it was the neighbor's trash can she had seen and not a giant wild cat, but I did not want to argue the point.

To this day, she still brings it up, how she endured that commute, morning after morning, braving lack of sleep and icy roads and, yes, even maneuvering around a mountain lion in our cul-de-sac.

I have tried to inject some rationality into her story. Like how her car's headlights may have thrown a weird shadow as she navigated the winding road. Or that mountain lions are not indigenous to Whidbey Island, and that to get there, one would have to cross the only bridge, a narrow, five-hundred-foot-high span over Deception Pass.

"There's also the ferry," she reminds me. "Which runs twice a day."

That is twice as many chances for a mountain lion to hop aboard and cruise on over. At least, that's what I am assuming her argument is. Anyway, facts shmacts. She knows what she saw. And the real fact was that Annmarie was running on fumes to be both a good teacher for her students and to be there for me.

My job could be pretty brutal as well. Being an EP-3 pilot meant deploying to remote locations—one plane, one crew—often without the ability to contact loved ones back home. I spent many holidays and birthdays away, hoping Annmarie wasn't too lonely, wishing I could tell her what we were doing and how much it mattered.

It hit me especially hard one Christmas Eve on a remote airbase in the middle of the Indian Ocean. I found myself in church singing hymns with a handful of other pilots and airmen, none of us able to make eye contact because of how heartsick we all were.

Sometimes, I wondered how folks pulled this off with kids at home. I had plenty of Navy buddies who tried. I never understood how they did it. The sad truth was that many did not. Divorce was an occupational hazard. And with Annmarie and I working so hard at our jobs and our marriage, we never even considered adding kids to our busy lives. It wasn't even a conversation—we just knew we were not having them.

As tough as it was, the missions made the time away worthwhile. I knew the work I was doing mattered. I had a purpose. Some of the most intense moments were during sorties against China, collecting intelligence on their military activities, especially when sabers rattled across the Taiwan Strait. When one of my squadron's planes was forced to crash land inside China after colliding with one of their fighters, I commanded the first reconnaissance mission launched in response. In spite of the tensions between the two countries, our president was determined to show that the United States would not be intimidated.

I flew missions the world over, from monitoring the Demilitarized Zone separating North and South Korea to patrolling the no-fly zones over Iraq during Saddam Hussein's reign of terror. In the days following the 9/11 attacks, I ferried an EP-3 halfway around the world to prepare for the invasion of Afghanistan. Those missions, and the purpose they gave me, sustained me during the long months away.

Whenever I was home between deployments, I did my best to be there for Annmarie. We made it work, even if that meant commuting two hours each way over roads littered with mountain lions. Then, one day, Annmarie brought me a map.

"You know you're a pilot, right?" she asked.

"Last time I checked," I said.

"Well, there's an airfield right . . . here," she said, pressing her finger into the map. "It's thirty minutes from my school, even with traffic. Why not fly to work?"

And so I did. We moved out of our separate residences and into a cozy house with a view of the Olympic Mountains across the sound. We were ideally situated, right next to the airfield she pointed out on the map with a straight shot down the highway to her school. Annmarie no longer had to wake up in the dead of night, and from time to time, I rented a Cessna for the fifteen-minute hop across Skagit Bay. Best of all, we lived in the same house. We did not have to divide our things between two places. When I was home, we shared our lives together—right down to shampoo and socks (Annmarie drew the line at toothbrushes).

HOUND AND SHADOW

There was one unexpected side effect of finally being in the same place. Annmarie felt my absences more than ever. Unlike before, when she stayed in her rented room, she had no housemates. When I was away, our home felt empty. Our first Christmas there together, she gave me a small metal bowl, roughly the size of an ashtray.

"What's this?" I said.

"It's a bowl," she said, grinning.

"It's very nice," I said. "What do you want me to do with it?"

"I want a dog," she said.

I turned the bowl over in my hands. Annmarie had grown up in a cat family. This bowl was, at best, big enough for a very small cat or a gerbil.

"Okay," I said. "But not a yip-yap dog. I want a big one, a dog that's built to do something. And, um, we'll need a real bowl."

Two days later, we were at the pound. I found my dog right away, a six-month-old black lab mix. In the twenty minutes I spent with him in the yard, he would not leave my side. When I crouched down, he leaned against me so hard that I repeatedly fell over. His old family said he was "too full of energy," so they dropped him off at the shelter. Apparently, he had chewed on things around their house. At six months, he was already big, but he was still a puppy at heart. *Of course he's full of energy*, I thought. *That's how puppies are.* Having grown up with dogs, I knew he just needed attention and space to run. Annmarie and I could give him that.

As were getting ready to leave, we walked past the chain-link kennels full of homeless dogs. Some cowered in their corners, while others barked angrily. But one stood out. A brindled hound with floppy ears leapt up and let out a bellowing woof. It was not angry or mean, just a big-dog "hello." Annmarie stopped, nose-to-nose with this happy hound standing on his hind legs.

"Who's this?" she asked the manager.

"No name," the manager said. "We found him in a parking lot a couple weeks ago. Today's his last day."

"What do you mean?" Annmarie said.

"I mean we have more dogs than we can care for. If they don't get adopted, we have to put them down," the woman replied. Annmarie looked horrified.

"This dog is coming with us," she said.

And so Shadow and Hound became unlikely brothers. We brought them home and settled in. And after they ran away repeatedly, overturned and ate an entire pot of chicken soup, chewed my snorkeling mask, our coffee table, and every one of my tennis shoes, we felt more like a family than ever before. We had purpose and adventure, and in spite of the oceans that often separated us, Annmarie and I had each other.

After three years, when my tour of duty was up, we felt a huge sense of satisfaction—and relief. We thought we had weathered the toughest challenge that marriage could throw our way.

I got my pick of assignments, and so Annmarie and I relocated to Charleston, South Carolina, where I taught naval history at The Citadel. I figured we were due for some real, uninterrupted time together.

It was the only assignment of my Navy career that afforded me free time. My workday was eight hours long, and if the wind was blowing when I left the office, I headed to the beach to kitesurf. Annmarie worked a bit harder than me (she always has), but we still had more evenings and weekends together than ever before.

Our marriage could not have been better. We had purpose: Annmarie teaching at a tough high school, me grooming naval officers in training. But after a few years of this, we discovered we wanted something more. During one of our evening strolls through the gaslit alleys in old town Charleston, Annmarie challenged me to a game. She would name a restaurant we had eaten at since living in South Carolina, and I would answer back with a different one. What began as a friendly memory contest morphed into an appalling awareness. When we hit the hundredth restaurant, we were surprised. By the time we hit two hundred, we were horrified. Who had that much time (and money) to go to that many restaurants? We had become like the married couples we swore we'd never be. We worked, went to movies, and ate out. We had a lot of fun, but was that all we wanted? Was this all we were going to do with the rest of our lives?

Three months later, Annmarie was pregnant. After months of soul-searching and many long conversations, I decided to leave the Navy. I applied and was accepted to law school, and soon we were on our way to Connecticut for another adventure with our brand new bundle of joy.

> *We had a lot of fun, but was that all we wanted? Was this all we were going to do with the rest of our lives?*

9 | Never Sail into a Harbor You Can't Sail out Of

3: Welcome to the Dropout Factory

Katie was, by far, our worst baby. Perhaps the worst baby ever, unless you count that creature the guy gave birth to in the original *Alien* film or that bedraggled zombie-eyed baby doll from *Toy Story 3*. Our sweet little first-born terror could have given them both a run for their money. She was NOT a bundle of joy.

That is what we tell ourselves, anyway. The truth is that *we* were the worst. We were the bedraggled zombies. We were the aliens. Despite college degrees and wilderness skills, Ken and I had little clue how to be parents. We figured out how to pick her up, but we could not set her down. Katie cried every time I put her in the bouncy seat, the stroller, the bassinet, or the crib, so I just held her. All the time. I carried her so much that I needed a wrist brace. I was seldom more than twenty feet away from my bathroom, but still, I went days without showers. I could not be in there alone without her wailing. I held her on my lap when I peed.

Ever the problem-solver, Ken theorized that the child was unhappy. He narrowed the causes of her disquiet to three possibilities: food, rest, or a dirty diaper. Ken chose to confront the butt end of the problem, so he changed her. All the time. We routinely went through twenty diapers a day, sometimes more. The cycle went like this: Katie cried, so I nursed her. But she fell asleep in a dirty diaper, so Ken changed her. Of course, she then woke up and fussed. So I nursed her again. And then she pooped again. So Ken changed her again. Which made her cry. So I nursed her . . . We went round and round. And the poor kid never got to sleep.

In fact, sleep was the kicker for all of us. No one was getting enough. Not even close. We were becoming more nutso with every passing day. Ken and I broke the night into shifts. I did the midnight feeding and woke again for the 5:00 a.m. He did the 2:30 a.m. feeding and was on call at 7:30 a.m. if she awoke before he left for work. But that merely ensured that neither of us ever got more than four or five hours of sleep at a stretch. Prior to Katie, I had been no stranger to sleep deprivation. In college, I was the girl in the computer lab writing papers at 2:00 a.m. When Ken and I were dating, I routinely drove all night just to visit him for a day. And even after we got married, our commutes necessitated waking at ridiculous o'clock to beat Seattle traffic. But for every crummy night's sleep, I always knew there was a lazy Saturday morning or a Sunday afternoon nap when I could recharge.

This is not the case when you have an infant. I remember sitting on the edge of my bed one night with my tush on the mattress and my feet dangling toward the carpet below. I could not remember whether I was waking up to feed the baby or going back to sleep because the baby had just been fed. So I sat there, too tired and confused to choose. Another night, I told Ken that I understood why some animals ate their young. Even days were foggy. I tried making pancakes with breastmilk but settled on ice cream for breakfast instead. Of course, I mistakenly put the half gallon of ice cream back in the pantry rather than the freezer. Later that day, I cried when I discovered the melted goop on the cereal shelf but then rallied when I realized I could probably use it to make the pancakes I'd abandoned earlier.

Looking back, it all seems so terribly funny. Because, eventually, of course, a baby learns to sleep. All babies learn to sleep. And then parents get to rest again. Sort of. But at the time, when Katie was a new baby and I was a new mom, it felt like our world would never be restored to balance again.

Ken did his best to be helpful through it all. But what they do not mention to you during your wedding ceremony or your baby shower or your engagement party is how you are going to look into the eyes of your beloved and want to punch him in the face after you have a child together. Yes, our affection for each other grew, and we were so much more in love than ever before when we gazed upon our (rarely) sleeping child. But I also kind of hated Ken. Because the inequity of childbirth is real. Men simply do not have the honor/horror of incubating a child. They do not get to experience the wonder/terror of childbirth as an active participant. Thus, both the before baby and after baby are quite different for them.

Within a day of our being home from the hospital, Ken was able to resume his fitness routine. I had to sit on a plastic donut to eat at the dinner table. Within a week, he was back at work, joking with colleagues, wearing clean clothes, and resuming his professional career path. Meanwhile, I smelled like old milk and wore the same pajama pants day and night. Ken's life returned to normal quite quickly, but it took me months to figure out what my new normal even was. Of course, there were inequities for him, too. Despite all his efforts, Katie cried more when he held her. And after a rough night with the baby, he had to get up and go to work, while I got to stay on maternity leave and watch television. I loved my husband for this gift of time with baby Katie. But I also resented him for it. I was slow to warm to the idea that imbalance was, in fact, its own kind of balance.

I loved my husband for this gift of time with baby Katie. But I also resented him for it.

In the rare moments when I was not sleepy or pissed off, I was soul-searching. Over the previous

4 IMBALANCE IS BALANCE

Love for this baby may have ruined our previous plans, but that same love enabled us to devise a new one.

 **2** Love Ruins Plans

seven years, Ken and I had been a happily married couple. We'd had adventures. We toured Israel, ate our way across Italy, and sailed the Ionian Sea. We'd had purpose. I taught tough kids and assisted low-income families with the college admissions process. Ken had flown reconnaissance missions and mentored young men and women considering a life of military service. Suddenly, everything we knew and loved about ourselves—and one another—was turned upside down. I did not want him flying over hostile territory anymore. We had a baby to think of. He did not want me breaking up fights and grading papers until eleven o'clock at night. We were a dad and a mom now. We had to live differently. Love for this baby may have ruined our previous plans, but that same love enabled us to devise a new one. Ken left the Navy and went to law school. I extended my childcare leave indefinitely and decided to embrace the life of a stay-at-home mom.

Except I had some problems.

I quickly realized that I did not know what it was that a stay-at-home mom did while she stayed-at-home. I remember my own mother cooking a lot, cleaning a little, attending meetings, and going to church. But I had trouble doing any of those things. Every time we went to the grocery store, Katie started screaming before I was even out of the produce aisle. I usually came home with apples, lettuce, and a box of cookies from the bakery (I made sure to get those first). We ate a lot of takeout that first year with Katie. The only opportunity I had to clean house was when she was asleep, but that was also the only time I had to eat, sleep, read, comb my hair, do laundry, or cry about how much I hated cleaning.

I did manage to take Katie for some walks. She hated her stroller.

I put her in it anyway—and inevitably ended up pushing it empty and wearing her in a baby carrier. Sometimes we wandered over to the park. It had a playground and a couple picnic tables. Katie was too little to do anything there. But it was still a destination. A goal. A reason to get out of the house. Unlike my mom, I had no meetings or church events. And since taking Katie anywhere was such a pain, we often just stayed home. I had a college degree and years of work and life experiences. And now I sat on the floor with my baby. Holding a rattle. Feeling trapped.

Another part of my problem was that I did not know any other moms. We had just moved to Connecticut. Ken was in school full time. I figured all the other stay-at-home moms were doing what I was doing: *staying at home.* Heck, it was in the job title. But I also thought there must be some way to find them. Couldn't we at least sit on the floor and shake rattles together? Ken's law school classmates were nearly all single or married with no children. And while they were really cool people, I felt like a gelatinous blob next to those high-powered law school gals. They had career aspirations. I had yoga pants—and miniature chocolate bars stashed throughout my house. I needed a like-minded posse.

I had never conducted a Google search for friends before. But I answered a message on a meeting board late one night and set out the next morning to meet my new Internet mommy crew at a shopping mall on the edge of town.

We convened at the food court. Five women, six babies—one of the gals had twins—and a tiny Chihuahua in a purse-like carrier. The mom explained he was a service dog named French Fry, and she fed him pretzel bites while her baby slept. We maneuvered our strollers around a group of tables in the quiet

> *I answered a message on a meeting board late one night and set out the next morning to meet my new Internet mommy crew.*

5 | TALK TO STRANGERS

corner, away from the coin-operated kids' rides and the guy handing out samples of orange chicken. At first, we talked mostly about tattoos. One of the moms had a different tat for each of her babies' daddies. I thought that was nice. Inclusive. The skull with a rose was not my personal taste, but I still respected the artistry. We also discussed pageants—which were the best to enter, which ones to avoid. Nearly everyone agreed that "blonde judges discriminated." Though against whom or because of what, I never quite followed. One mom thought it was better to get a baby's modeling career started in print magazines. That had been her nine-month-old's route, and she had already modeled twice for Sears. But another mommy insisted that television advertising was the only way to really make a living at it. That was why she and her daughter were taking the bus to California after Christmas. I looked at my baby Katie, still in her green footie pajamas, and wondered whether I had a pageant winner or merely a third alternate on my hands.

I had never felt so inept at small talk. But these were my people now, so I tried hard to keep up, nodding when other women nodded, laughing when they laughed, too. After an hour or so, most of the gals had to go. They had roots to dye and figurines to exchange at the Hallmark store. Plus, for those with "scheduled children," it was getting close to naptime. I lingered with the last gal, Allison, deciding that once she left, I would go and order a second chocolate cupcake from the stand nearby. I had earned it. Plus, I had nowhere I needed to be.

But Allison did not leave either, and I will forever remember her for that. These days, we live far apart, and both of us have had several more children. But back then, she was my first stay-at-home friend. Neither of us quite knew what this mommy gig was supposed to be, but we were smart enough to realize that we did not have a great handle on it yet. We ate our cupcakes and strolled through the mall and made a date to hang out again the following Thursday. Together, we learned the building blocks and not-so-secret activities of the stay-at-home-parent world— library story time, baby sign language class, the weekly Raffi sing-a-long at the Episcopal church. Sometimes, we just hung out at my house or hers—usually hers, because it was cleaner and dog-free—and we drank tea and laughed and commiserated about how much harder this was than we'd expected. And though Allison's family relocated to North Carolina a few months after she and I met, because of her friendship, I gained a toehold in Mommyland. I met more moms—Jennifer, Michal, Yasmine, and Kelly. Moms who, to this day, are kindred spirits and treasured friends. I still felt bonkers a lot of the time, but so, it seemed, did a lot of other parents. I was in good company.

Back to School

But then there was that one Wednesday. Katie and I had stopped for gelato after our mother-baby fitness class when I saw the article in the paper. The Yale Graduate School was accepting applications for a new teacher-training program. Participants would complete intensive course-work, receive job placement in an area high school, and earn a master's in urban education from the university. The only hitch: you had to be willing to work with tough kids.

My palms started to sweat, like an addict in need of a fix. I had to get into that program. This was a sign. I needed to teach again. It wasn't like I hadn't tried being a stay-at-home mom. I had given it my best shot. But other moms seemed so much better at it. They were practically fluent in baby sign language. I had only mastered three gestures—"more," "thank you," and "dinosaur." They breastfed proudly in public places, while I preferred to hide in bathroom stalls or my car. Other parents read avidly about baby safety and baby nutrition and baby learning. I still spent a lot of time on the floor with that rattle. Plus, this was a chance to reestablish the balance in our marriage. Ken was in grad school; I would be in grad school. Ken was pursuing his career; I would pursue my career. We would split this parenting gig fifty-fifty, just like we used to share household responsibilities before we had a baby.

I wanted to go home and complete the application that night. But it took me several months to compile the necessary forms, transcripts, reference letters, and essays. My GRE scores had expired, so I retook those exams, along with several others the teaching program required. Katie's naptime became standardized test preparation. It had been years since I wrote a timed essay or narrowed down multiple-choice responses. At first, I was not entirely sure I could relearn the material for the application deadline. But with each set of practice questions, my dusty brain felt nimbler. It was good to have another daily purpose.

It feels miserable to admit this, but looking back, being "just a mom" was not enough for me. I wanted a professional path. Instead, I had been sidelined by diapers and wipes. I know some people might view this as unforgivable. What greater gift is there than to care for our children? But I could not do it all the time. Well, maybe I could. But I did not want to. To their credit, none of my mommy friends ever made me feel bad about my decision to go back to school and back to work. I do not actually think the Mommy Wars exist like you hear about in the news. Most parents are just muddling through, trying to figure out how to balance work and home, personal growth and growth for their children. At that time, what I needed was to put on pants that buttoned, take a shower daily, and leave the house *by myself* to do something unrelated to raising a family. I needed to be more than just Katie's mom.

When the program director at Yale phoned me for an interview, I nearly changed my mind. It was one thing to fill out forms and mail papers to a post office box, but was I really going to abandon my child so I could spend time with other people's children? Did that even make any sense? So what if full-time parenting was not my favorite? Katie was a year old now. She needed me. Katie's godmother, Jen, talked me off of the ledge. She reminded me that millions of mothers before me had agonized over the work-life balance. My meltdown was neither terribly original nor well timed. I had not even been admitted to the program yet. They did not need to hear all of my angst and kvetching at the interview. And,

Jen said, even if I was accepted, I could always say, "No, thanks." I got my courage up, swallowed back my crazy, and decided to take the plunge. I had two weeks to prepare.

Step One: I tackled my appearance. I went to a new stylist the next day and got what turned out to be an egregious haircut. I had been going for Young Professional but ended up with Just Out of Shock Treatment. Undeterred, I hit a department store and bought a tailored black jacket and an alarmingly large-sized blue blouse—none of my previous dress shirts would button over my still ridiculously large mommy boobs. I looked like someone who might ring your doorbell in the middle of the day offering to sell you a new life insurance policy or maybe a vacuum cleaner, but this was still a step in the right direction. At least I was wearing shoes.

Step Two: I practiced interviewing. Ken quizzed and cross-examined me during our evening walks around the neighborhood. We discovered that fidgety Katie would actually sit in the stroller if we put her dinner on the plastic tray. Not snacks—she flew through raisins and crackers way too quickly. We provided her with a multi-course meal: chicken, steamed veggies, pasta, fruit, and several supplemental toys to keep her occupied enough to let us mock-interview in peace.

With Katie settled, Ken would begin by asking me broad-sweeping and/or preposterous questions. I would practice answering with an unflappability and panache that I did not actually possess. It usually went something like this:

Ken: If asked to take over as an administrator of a high school tomorrow, what would you change on your first day?

Me: (Dramatic pause.) Nothing.

Ken: You mean to tell me that you would walk into a failing school and not do anything to right that sinking ship?

Me: That's right. On my first day, I would listen, observe, and question. But I would not change anything. I think the mistake we often make when considering underperforming schools is the administration of treatment before diagnosis of the ailment. We are quick to try to fix without understanding what is broken.

Ken would usually interrupt at this point to ask a follow-up or throw me a curveball. "Which major league baseball player most influences your teaching style?" or "Who is your favorite eighteenth-century poet?" Whether I referenced William Blake or Babe Ruth made no difference to Ken. He liked trying to rattle me, and I appreciated the chance to think on my feet.

No matter if we practiced one question or twelve, we always ended with the same one:

Ken: What would you say is your biggest weakness as a teacher?

Me: (With feeling.) I give too much.

I had been asked this question years ago in an interview for a teaching fellowship in college, and I overshared. For about a third of that thirty-minute session, I catalogued my weaknesses: competitiveness, stubbornness, a relentless need to be right, difficulty being on time, trouble with rules and authority . . . I had thought my openness would impress the college interviewer, but if it did, it impressed upon him the need to give that fellowship to someone else. Likely someone with fewer "authority issues" and an ability to be on time for work. Ken had humorously consoled me that day by brainstorming a dozen better answers to that weakness question—all of which were technically strengths. "You put in long hours to make sure the work meets your unnecessarily high standards," he said. "You care so much it hurts." Now,

On the day of the interview, I donned my jacket and blouse and stuffed two extra nursing pads in my bra.

7 CHANGE YOUR SOCKS

all these years later, Ken still liked to tease me by ending our practice interviews with the question he knew gave me trouble. With his harping, I knew I would not panic into too much honesty, like admitting, "I don't always remember to brush my teeth in the morning."

On the day of the interview, I donned my jacket and blouse and stuffed two extra nursing pads in my bra in case I got so nervous that my breastmilk started to leak. On the drive downtown, I sang '80s tunes to warm up my voice and settle the jitters. I felt pretty sure that no one else's pre-interview fluff song was "(You Gotta) Fight for Your Right (to Party!)" by the Beastie Boys.

Then I walked through those doors and got myself a ticket to graduate school.

FACTORY WORK

A 2007 study by Johns Hopkins University identified James Hillhouse High School as one of the nation's "dropout factories" (Heintz 2007). Three out of every five students who entered Hillhouse as freshmen never made it to graduation day. This was the high school into which the graduate program placed me. We had metal detectors and security guards. We had gang members and fights. Every so often, a teacher's car got stolen and ended up being sold for spare parts. But, thankfully, most of the nonsense occurred outside of the classroom. Inside, well, that's where the magic happened. Because in a school like Hillhouse, nobody was really making the kids attend class. There were so many truant students that if someone wanted to skip, it was usually a couple of weeks before he or she would even get caught. Sometimes, there was no penalty at all. In the end, the only kids who came to class were the ones who really wanted to be there. There was something great about that.

Willa Cather once said, "Most of the basic material a writer works with is acquired before the age of fifteen." My fourth-period writing workshop confirmed that. We wrote every single day, and the kids' stories were both heartbreaking and beautiful. Two students had recently lost their mothers, one to AIDS, another to murder. Two students had fathers who were incarcerated. Every single child in the class was suspended at least once that year, even the gal who was pregnant. They complained about having to write every day. But, usually, they did it anyway. And I wrote alongside them. I learned to share more of my story.

I had great professors at Yale and terrific colleagues at Hillhouse. From Jack and Linda, Simon, Jessica, Wendy, Susan, Ben, and John, I learned to be a facilitator, a participant, and a student of my students. I helped them shape their anger, joy, and sorrow into finished stories. We were all wrestling with feelings of disconnect between who we wanted to be and who we felt like we were. My students dealt with anger and grief that came from growing up without a mother or father—or both. Some believed their childhoods had been stolen from them, that they had been forced to grow up too soon and to take on adult responsibilities while they were still young. Others had difficulty trusting adults, since grown-ups had let them down repeatedly. I left my own daughter in daycare so I could be in class with these kids. Occasionally, I pictured Katie as a teenager, writing stories about how her mother had pushed her away to go back to work. But most of the time, I knew that Katie was well cared for in her school and my students were well cared for in mine.

Early in my program, I took a full load of graduate courses and taught high school part time, so it was not unusual to have exceedingly long days. I quickly learned that it was tricky to be both a parent and a student. When we had group projects and folks wanted to meet from seven to ten o' clock at night, all I could think was that I would be missing bedtime. I liked my grad school classmates, but I felt distant from them. I was the only one who was married—the only one with a child. They were pricing Christina Aguilera tickets, and I was recording *The Wiggles* to watch with Katie on Sunday mornings. I remember feeling torn between advocating for my needs as a parent and being taken seriously as a student. It seemed like I could not do both.

In the beginning, I actually explained that it was tough for me to be away from my daughter and that I did not want to talk much about her when I was in class. I wanted to *do school*. I did not want her creeping into my teacher world. Later, especially when I was at Hillhouse full time, I learned that some of the best moments occurred in the overlap between my home and work life. Katie came with me when I brought my students to tour a nearby college. She sat and colored in my classroom when I had work to finish after her daycare had let out for the day.

There were plenty of times when I did not feel very good at being a teacher, a student, a mother, and a wife. I was always juggling, never quite settling into one role. As I struggled to find that tricky balance between home and work, implementing new teaching strategies and staying true to what I knew, I flailed about quite a bit. I nearly flunked a class, which would have resulted in losing my fellowship. During our summer semester, I received some of the first negative ratings I'd ever gotten as a teacher. It was a weird time. Three years prior, I had been voted teacher of the year at Eastside Catholic High School in Washington State. I had given speeches, earned a National Board Certification, and been awarded a fellowship by the National Endowment for the Humanities. But now, trying to be both a mom and a student, a teacher and a learner, I sometimes felt like I was failing at all of it.

But then there were those other days. When things just clicked. When I drafted an entire paper in my head during an evening stroller/dinner walk. When I reframed a difficult student, saw stubbornness as stick-to-it-ness and weaknesses as strengths. When I implemented a strategy in the classroom—like Socratic discussions or breakout sessions on race, gender, and class—and kids' eyes opened a little wider. Those were great days when it all came together.

When one of my students won an essay contest addressing the proliferation of gun violence in the neighborhood, our class was invited to a local radio station to be interviewed. As soon as we got on air, it became clear that my kids were supposed to talk about how bad things were at their school. But they refused to be pigeonholed by the interviewer. Instead, they expressed pride. "Just because our school doesn't look great on the outside, that doesn't mean it isn't great on the inside. Our teachers care about us. We look out for one another. At Hillhouse, we are a family."

And it was true.

I still worried occasionally that I was letting Katie down and not being the mother she needed. But I knew Ken and her teachers nurtured her, and I was becoming the professional I wanted to be and the teacher that my students needed. I was not a replacement for the folks who raised them at home. But I was the woman who supported them during the day, just like Ms. Stephanie and Ms. Colleen tended to my Katie at daycare.

For a child to make it through times of crisis, it is said that he or she just needs one person. One person who will listen to her story. One person who will take his call. For some of those students at James Hillhouse High School, I was that person. It was imbalanced and difficult, but it was worth missing my own child. The dropout factory was a transformative place for students and educators alike. It reawakened my purpose and assured me it was okay to be both a teacher and a mom.

4: Skype-Parenting from Kabul

Eventually, Annmarie and I did emerge from the hazy half sleep of our first months as new parents. Katie grew and flourished, Annmarie found her path back to teaching, and I was finally able to observe the world from the new perspective of a dad with a child. I noticed that I had a pretty great gig. Everywhere I went, people congratulated me. Even my mess-ups were endearing, like forgetting to comb Katie's hair or leaving her in jammies all day. As a dad, I could do no wrong.

For what little work I had done to create this tiny person, I sure was getting an undue share of the credit. Annmarie never got such consideration. The double standard was egregious at times, a fact she first noticed when we were in graduate school together. On the rare occasions when Annmarie was late to class because of Katie (getting barf out of clothes adds a few minutes to the morning routine), teachers and classmates were less forgiving. Even her female peers were hard on her. The message seemed to be that if she couldn't handle being both a mom and a student, then maybe she should choose just one role, not two.

My experience was altogether different. Not only did I show up late to class because of my kid—sometimes I brought her with me. Far from being judged, I was admired. My highly visible struggles (and failures) at balancing these competing parts of my life were seen as noble. Being a dad while working my way through law school wasn't a conflict. To peers and professors alike, it was catnip. They adored the notion of a father juggling both at once, so having a kid on my lap during constitutional law class made me Dad of the Year. We can talk all we want about *leaning in*, but if you are a woman, the message seemed to be that there had better not be a baby holding you back.

Wherever possible, Annmarie and I took advantage of the double standard. Once again, we found balance in the imbalance. While she battened down the hatches to finish her master's in urban education, I became the worst (and happiest) law student in history. When I needed to bring Katie to class with me, we developed a routine. We arrived a few minutes early to lay out a space with sheets of poster paper, then we lined up her crayons. While I took notes, Katie did her work. Occasionally, she'd whisper something in my ear, and classmates would smile dotingly in our direction.

I typically handled the little stuff, too, the doctor's appointments and trips to the zoo. I noticed the same thing everywhere I went. Dads always seem to get the benefit of the doubt. Like with socks. I have never been good at matching them. In fact, clothing in general is not my strong suit. So whenever I got Katie dressed for a public outing, she looked like a little clown. "How lovely," people said.

This drove Annmarie nuts. "You know what people would think if I did that?" she asked.

"That you had no fashion sense," I replied.

"No," she said. "They'd think I was a bad mother."

I once took Katie, shoeless and coatless, to the grocery store in the middle of winter. I did remember socks, but they were definitely mismatched. It was a quick trip, and I carried her from our car to the store and plopped her straight into the shopping cart seat. We got our sundries and headed toward the checkout. A woman tapped me on the elbow.

"I noticed your child doesn't have shoes," she said.

Here it comes, I thought. *The bad-parent lecture.*

"It must be hard, doing what you do," she said. "It's so beautiful to see a father spending time with his little girl." She paused then said, "I'd like to buy you some shoes . . . and a coat . . . and I could give you a ride back home, or . . . wherever you need to go."

By "wherever you need to go," I'm fairly certain she meant the homeless shelter where we apparently had come from.

"Thank you so much," I said. "But we're okay. Our car is right over there. I'll make sure to keep her warm."

I interpreted this encounter as a commentary on the kindness of strangers. Also, as a statement about how shabbily I dress ("hoboesque," my wife says). But when I got home and recounted the episode to Annmarie, she had a wholly different take.

"This woman offered to buy you shoes?" she asked.

"Well, for Katie, anyway," I said.

"And she told you how awesome it was that you were spending time with your daughter?"

"Yeah," I said. I knew I was in trouble but was not yet sure why.

"If I had carried a half-naked kid through a snow-covered parking lot," she said, "someone would have reported me to CPS."

I gave her a blank look, the one that says *I don't know what's coming next, so you keep talking.*

"See, you don't even know what CPS is!" she said. "It's Child Protective Services. And when dads bring their kids to class with hair uncombed and faces covered in dirt or drag them through a blizzard with bare feet and no coat, it's endearing . . ."

I interrupted. "It wasn't a blizzard. And she had socks on."

"Not the point!" Annmarie said. "If I did that as a mom, I'd have the kid taken away from me."

"That's an option?" I said.

The more I thought about it, and the more I observed, the more I

realized how right Annmarie was. Once I began looking, the double standard was everywhere. I did things with Katie that should have gotten me
fired from being a dad. On trips to the grocery store, I let her hang on to
the shopping cart axle and drag behind like a mop. She loved it. People
thought it was funny. I often carried her, in public, upside down by one
foot. She wasn't heavy, and it freed my other hand for opening car doors
or loading groceries. Mostly, I loved to hear her giggle. I got away with
things like that. When I tried to picture Annmarie doing the same thing,
all I could see were the dirty looks followed by a quick trip to bad-mom-
my prison.

So, yeah, I had a pretty sweet deal as a new dad. The imbalance was
tremendous, but even within the disparity, Annmarie and I found balance, and we settled into a routine we were all happy with. As long as,
every so often, I acknowledged that dads can turn their babies into human
mops and be high-fived for it while moms cannot mismatch socks without going to jail.

Phoning It In

The funny thing about balance is that it is tough to maintain. As soon
as we found our stride and figured out how to make our little pooping,
eating, sleeping, crying thing happy, we began to get restless again.

By the end of my second semester in law school, I knew I needed
something more. My service in uniform seemed like a lifetime ago. In
fact, it had not been that long. But with every passing day, the military
pilot I had been faded further and further into the distance. On my last
day in the Navy, I had a premonition about this. I was sitting at the
out-processing clerk's desk, about to sign my DD214, the piece of paper
that would officially end my time in the service. I stared at the form in
front of me, its empty signature block beckoning. One quick stroke of the
pen, and I would be a civilian. Law school awaited, and beyond that, an
entire future in which I could define my own path. And yet I hesitated.

I knew it was the right call for me and my family. But I also knew I was signing away an important part of who I was and that I might regret it someday.

Throughout law school, I found myself contemplating that signature and what it meant. I was a parent and a student now. That was it. Most days, I enjoyed being a (mostly) stay-at-home dad. But I longed for the sense of purpose I had in uniform. And when it came to adventure, my life had none. Unless you counted middle-of-the-night feedings or mad scrambles to get to church on time.

When a friend approached about an opportunity to serve as a human rights consultant in Afghanistan, I jumped at the chance. The job sounded simple enough. Travel to Afghanistan via Pakistan, link up with a group of leading intellectuals and influencers, recruit more, and convince them to convene in Kabul. Their goal: to discuss strategies for seeking redress against war criminals, including Taliban commanders and other warlords.

Most of my close friends were still in uniform. Many, including some of my former students, were serving in Iraq and Afghanistan. My motivation for accepting the job rested on a couple things. I missed the sense of purpose the Navy had given me. I missed the adrenaline rush of flying. More than anything, though, I thought about my friends, now serving during wartime while I sat comfortably within the ivory towers of Yale Law School.

I imagined Katie one day asking, "Daddy, what did you do in the war?"

At this point, my answer would be, "I stayed at home . . . and changed diapers."

It was not an ideal time for me to leave the country. Annmarie's graduate program ran through the summer. If I left, she would be a single mother and a full-time student. I love a lot of things about my wife—her curvy hips and her curly hair, the way she can match me stride for stride in a 5K and destroy me on the tennis court. But most of all, I love her heart. She says yes to the world and finds a way to make even the most difficult circumstances seem possible. "I got this, babe," she assured me when I asked her about Afghanistan.

So I took the job.

Two months later, I was in Kabul, making preparations to travel across Afghanistan and rendezvous in secret with journalists, politicians, poets, and others. The country had been at war for decades, leaving an entire generation scarred by violence. My list of people to meet included any Afghan in a position of prominence. Anyone who might help bring the country one step closer to finding justice for the millions of victims of war crimes.

When I arrived, Kabul was a city on the brink. Every intersection was patrolled by heavily armed soldiers. Just a few weeks prior, the capital had erupted in riots against the American presence after a truck in a US military convoy lost control and plowed into a crowd of civilians. In planning for my trip, I intentionally chose to go with a low profile. Most westerners traveled with heavy security. They felt safer, but all of that hardware made them targets. I went for the opposite tactic. I grew a convincing-enough beard (Annmarie hated it) and whenever possible stayed with ordinary Afghans. I wanted to get as far as possible from the westerners' heavily guarded compounds. Over the course of my travels, the strategy proved successful, both for maintaining my own safety and for gaining the confidence of the Afghans I had to win over. But my first wake-up in Kabul made me question everything.

The blast from the initial car bomb rocked me out of bed. I threw on clothes in case I needed to make a quick getaway. Peeling back the curtain, I peered into the street below. Several blocks away, a thick column of black smoke rose skyward. People stared in the direction of the commotion. Then a second bomb went off, and another column of smoke joined the first. After a moment's hesitation, pedestrians and street traffic continued as before. For me, their nonchalance was as disorienting as the attack itself.

I soon learned not to overreact to such things. Car bombs happened all the time, and they often came in pairs (rarely threes). This time, the primary target was a busload of police recruits. The second blast was meant for the emergency responders. I don't know how many were killed (I lost count of the number of attacks while I was there), but when I drove past the scene later that day, the wall by the road was splattered with blood and pockmarked with shrapnel. It stayed that way for months. That was my welcome to Afghanistan.

Back in the Navy, the combat reconnaissance missions I had flown happened thirty thousand feet above the fray. That was a comfortable way to spend a war, especially when compared to what front-line ground units were up against. My mission to Afghanistan was unlike anything I had faced as a pilot. Though I was never directly in the line of fire, I came to see the evil of the war in ways I never imagined. I conducted dozens of interviews with victims of war crimes, including one with the parent of a child disfigured by Taliban agents. She had been attending a girls' school, which was newly reopened since the fall of the Taliban. As she walked home one day, two men roared up on a motorcycle. One opened a jar and threw the contents into her face. It was one of the hundreds of acid attacks that took place every year.

The assault left the child partly blind and one side of her face permanently scarred. This was punishment for wanting to learn to read. Also, it served as a warning to other parents who dared send their own girls to school. Every time I heard one of these stories, every time I spoke with a traumatized father, I thought about my own family. I thought, most of all, about Katie and how lucky we were to live in America.

Afghanistan is a backward country. On a scale of Modern to Medieval, it sits off the chart, somewhere to the left of Stone Age. Infant mortality is the highest on the planet. Pregnancy is the leading cause of death among women of child-bearing age (Harvey 2011). In rural Afghanistan, which is most of the country, social cohesion is maintained by ancient and unbending codes. In the Pashtun areas where the Taliban holds sway, the underlying characteristic of these strictures is the total subjugation of women. Time after time, I uncovered shocking examples of this, from women being stoned to death for "adultery" (accused, convicted, and sentenced without trial) to young girls being traded as brides in order to settle blood feuds between families. What I discovered did not give me much hope for Afghanistan achieving any semblance of justice.

My more honest interlocutors admitted as much. "There is no hope for war crimes trials here while we are still a country at war," they said. That brutal sentiment was captured most vividly in one of my last interviews. It was with a father who had a daughter a few years older than Katie. He was proud of his girl, a student in the local school. But that is not what I came to talk about. I wanted to learn about his brother, who was killed by the local warlord for some trivial offense. Rumor had it he had been crushed alive by a tank. Through my interpreter, I inquired as gently as I could. I wanted to know what kind of justice would seem fair for such a heinous act. The father waved the question off, scoffing at the very notion of "justice." Through his reaction, I finally understood the hard reality of living in a society still torn apart by conflict. This father hated the warlord who murdered his brother, but he wanted him to remain in power. The warlord was anti-Taliban and served as a stabilizing force. To this parent, it was more important that his daughter could walk to school unafraid of acid attacks than that his brother's killer be brought to justice.

For all of Afghanistan's backwardness, one modern feature stood out. The country, at least its urban centers, had surprisingly good Internet service. I did my best to avoid the more popular Internet cafés, a favorite target of suicide bombers, but whenever possible, I Skyped home. Back in the military, I developed a routine of focusing entirely on the mission at hand. I rarely called Annmarie then, which made me better at my job and allowed both of us to get into a battle rhythm. Annmarie taught, I flew, and the months sailed by. In Afghanistan, however, I did whatever I could to stay plugged into what was happening on the home front.

The difference, of course, was Katie. I had a little girl now. Even though I was halfway around the world, I wanted her to hear my voice. Annmarie would put her laptop on the floor. Katie would toddle over, touch the monitor, and make silly faces. But her attention span was brief, and she would turn back to her books and toys, leaving Annmarie and I face to face with the strangeness of our situation.

We have always been pretty honest with one another. From her first days teaching in Florida, Annmarie often shared her toughest students' stories with me. As a pilot returning from deployments, I told her about tangling with enemy fighters off China. But this was different. It was like telling her about an engine fire while it was happening. Calling home from Afghanistan let me see Katie and let her hear my voice, but it strained my relationship with my wife.

The toughest calls were when Annmarie was aggravated. She was parenting alone. She was tired. She had mushy peas in her hair. Did she really need to hear me talk about car bombs? I often held back because I wanted to spare her the added worry. Too many of our calls ended with the distance between us feeling even greater. Despite my attempts at parenting by Skype, Annmarie did all the heavy lifting, and I was not there for the big moments. That summer, Katie learned her ABCs and how to play hide and seek. She tried her first Thai food. She learned to love the ocean. I missed all of it. My time away impacted the father, and partner, I was able to be.

I cannot say for sure that I made any difference in Afghanistan. There is still so much turmoil in that part of the world. Was it worth being away from my family if I could not alleviate the suffering of another? In the end, I say yes. We can only teach our children who we are through what we do. When Katie asks me now what I did in the war, I can answer her faithfully. I sought to defend the weak and bring justice to the oppressed. I did this to the best of my ability. And whether Katie is on a playground or halfway around the world, this is a code we both can live by.

The Mission Continues

I came home from Afghanistan still searching. Some days, between class-es, I would wander across the street to a cemetery near the law school and sit next to the grave of a sergeant killed in Iraq. I did not know him. But it was as close as I could get to those of my buddies who died in uniform. Leaving the military, I made a promise to my wife that I would make the transition to civilian life. I did not want to miss seeing my daughter grow up. But I often thought about the thousands of other parents serving in Iraq and Afghanistan who carried that burden every day so I would not have to. Every minute I spent with Katie was paid for by the sacrifices of better men.

One of those better men was my college buddy, Eric Greitens, who went on to become a Navy SEAL. In early 2007, I got word that his bar-racks in Fallujah, Iraq, had been blown up by a suicide truck bomb. Mercifully, Eric survived, but he had to be medevacked back to the States. Meanwhile, I was surrounded by people who had no idea what was hap-pening in that part of the world. In my law school class of two hundred, there were only two other veterans. A forty-year-old ban on ROTC, dat-ing back to the Vietnam War, remained in effect (it was eventually lifted in 2011). To most students, the conflicts in Afghanistan and Iraq were afterthoughts at best.

What made this especially ironic was Yale's historically deep ties to the military and its once-proud tradition of sending graduates to fight for their country. One of the oldest buildings on campus was Memorial Hall, an auditorium dedicated to the memory of graduates killed in our nation's wars. On its interior stone walls are engraved the names of hun-dreds of alumni dating back to the Revolutionary War. At first glance, it is a sobering reminder of the cost of war, of the price paid by so many young men (there are no women honored as war dead on the walls of Yale's Memorial Hall—largely because Yale did not admit women until the late 1960s and because women continue to be underrepresented in front-line combat roles). But a closer look at the names tells another story. From WWI to WWII, through Korea and Vietnam, the men of Yale shouldered their share of the burden. For those conflicts, the list of war dead is heartbreakingly long. But in the last forty years, not a single name has been added. During the longest wars in our nation's history, those in Iraq and Afghanistan, the elites of Yale have been AWOL.

This disconnect between what my friends in uniform were going through and what my classmates at Yale were taking completely for granted became almost unbearable. I had few outlets for my frustration. I talked to friends still in the military. I occasionally wrote for NPR. Mostly, I just stewed. Then, one day, in the most innocent setting imaginable, my frustration boiled over.

I was sitting at a coffee shop outside the law school when a National Guard convoy rumbled past. In an attempt at humor, someone behind me said, "What, is there a war on?" I felt my anger welling up. I stood, spilling coffee across the table. I turned around, ready to explain to this spoiled-brat Ivy Leaguer that *YES, there is a war on, and good people are dying, and little girls are being mutilated for wanting to read, and justice will never be delivered, and so help me God, I'll put my fist through your smug little face if you say another word.* But as our eyes met, I realized that it wasn't this kid's fault. Yale was a bubble. There were plenty of others to blame for making it that way.

I paused long enough to let the emotion subside and walked past. I made my way to the cemetery, spent some time among the stones, and came to a realization. *There has to be a better way to honor those who have risked their lives so that I don't have to—so that I can be here with Katie.*

I called Eric, my Navy SEAL friend. He had just come back from Bethesda Naval Hospital, the facility where wounded Marines and Navy personnel recover upon returning to the United States. Eric said, "Ken, you have to go. You have to meet these men." I told Annmarie that I needed some time alone. She had her hands full with Katie and school, but she understood. Carrying around this anger, I was no use to either of them. I needed to change my own socks.

So I drove down to Washington, DC, alone. As I approached Bethesda, I was not sure what to expect. I assumed I would be the one offering words of encouragement to these broken young men. Instead, the opposite happened. One of them, about to be wheeled into his tenth reconstructive surgery, said this: "Sir, I lost my legs. That's it. I didn't lose my desire to serve or my pride in being an American."

Those Marines, some of them badly mangled, expressed such resolve that I had no choice but to be inspired. If they had one thing in common, besides being stuck in a military hospital, it was their irrepressible desire to continue serving. Almost every one of them wanted to get back to their units. For a lot of them, that wasn't possible. But what they really wanted was the chance to be useful again. More than anything, they craved a purpose.

Eric and I put our heads together and in a matter of weeks had the makings of a nonprofit we called The Mission Continues. We raised money, some from Eric's saved combat pay, and created a fellowship program. The idea was to enable returning vets to continue serving their communities and their country after they had taken off the uniform. While our explicit goal was to empower these extraordinary men and women, Eric and I also wanted to change the way Americans perceived them. Veterans did not need to be pitied or, worse, feared. They were assets, not liabilities. We wanted our fellow citizens, like my classmates at Yale, to see that veterans still had a great deal left to give.

By the following spring, The Mission Continues had a full head of steam. We had our first cohort of fellows, and the idea was working. Our veteran participants reported that the opportunity to serve again had a real impact on their path back to civilian life, and

I told Annmarie that I needed some time alone. She had her hands full with Katie and school, but she understood.

7 | CHANGE YOUR SOCKS

the nonprofits where they worked soon saw what incredible assets they were. One veteran worked on an equine therapy ranch, using horses to provide emotional and physical therapy to disabled kids. Another fellow worked as a peer support counselor with vets like himself at his local VA. Still another served as a mentor for troubled youth in her hometown.

Eric and I hired a small but capable team to run the program, but we still needed high-level leadership. As my graduation date approached, I faced a dilemma. I could play it safe and join a law firm. There, I would make more money than I ever had and would be able to afford whatever my family needed. Private schools, nannies, vacations—the works. Or I could redouble my efforts at The Mission Continues and help build it into an organization that could change the way veterans of my generation are viewed. I knew the right decision, but there was one big problem. The Mission Continues could barely afford to pay me. I would make maybe $1000 per month. Annmarie and I would both have to work extra to make up the difference. And there was no guarantee this start-up nonprofit would even succeed, which would leave me out of a job altogether.

I had a long talk with Annmarie. This decision, like the one to leave the Navy, had to be made by *both* of us. She summed it up this way: "So, you're going to give up a six-figure salary, work just as hard, *and* take a second job?"

"Yep," I said. "With you working, Katie and I can both be covered by your health care. We won't do vacations or presents for our anniversary or Christmas. And any dinners out will have to be at Kelly's Kone Konnection up the road."

"Okay," Annmarie said. "It'll be an adventure."

"Worth the mishaps?" I asked.

"Only one way to find out," she said. And then, as I knew she would, Annmarie told me to go for it.

Graduation day came, and I walked across that stage with Katie in my arms. When the dean handed me my diploma, Katie grabbed it and held it high over her head. With all the classes she had attended, I think

"Okay," Annmarie said. "It'll be an adventure."

"Worth the mis-haps?" I asked.

"Only one way to find out," she said.

I ADVENTURES ARE WORTH THE MISHAPS

she thought it was for her. The next day, I became the executive director of The Mission Continues. To make a little extra money, I lined up a teaching gig on the side, running a college seminar on the meaning of citizenship. It was right up my alley, a chance to educate young people about the responsibilities, and not just the rights, that go along with being part of any community.

I had the world in my hands: a job I loved with purpose and adventure and a family that supported me. When Annmarie discovered she was pregnant again, we even figured out how we could survive on less. We would rent out our Connecticut home, and with the little we had saved each month, we would take a family sabbatical at a tiny cottage on the Chesapeake. With another child on the way, a little girl we would call Elizabeth, life seemed too good to last. And it was.

The ultrasounds showed a perfectly healthy baby. Annmarie's doctors said everything was fine. But that perfect world I thought I held in my hands was about to be turned upside down.

5: Every Two to Three Hours

O f our three children, Lizzie's birth was the easiest. My contractions started midday. We got to the hospital around five o'clock. Ninety minutes later, this round little angel was sleeping in my arms. The whole thing was kind of a breeze.

It was only later that we discovered her birth had not gone quite as smoothly as we thought.

"We'll make sure you leave here with a list of specialists to call," said one well-intentioned nurse.

"Doctors have made such progress in this area," said another.

"The craniofacial liaison is on a leave of absence," said a young resident with spiky cool-guy hair. "Mind if I take a look?" He had a dirty mustard-yellow backpack slung over his shoulder that he set on the floor before washing his hands and shining a penlight into Lizzie's tiny mouth. He started speaking medical-ese—*z-furlough, maxillofacial,* and *PRS mandibular deficiency*—but I was most distracted by that backpack. I had never seen a doctor carrying one before. It seemed unprofessional. Was he a student? Were we his last stop for the night? Couldn't he have found a locker for his gym shoes and granola bars before he sauntered in here like some character from *Grey's Anatomy* to tell us our daughter had a birth defect?

With the excitement of a schoolboy, Cool Guy explained that he and his colleagues were going to surgically reconstruct my daughter's mouth and Eustachian tubes. And that it was going to be awesome. He did not use that word, "awesome," but that was his general tone. He was super psyched to tell us about this amazing procedure that they did now. We were lucky to have access to such spiffy medical treatment. Again, not his words, but that was the overall impression. He asked whether we had any questions. When we did not, he slung his musty bag over one shoulder and left.

To be fair, all of these folks had probably delivered news like this on many occasions. Maybe they thought telling us about all the treatment options available to our six-hour-old baby would be reassuring. And who doesn't want to know that Everything Is Going To Be All Right? Except I had just carried this child for nine months and given birth to her without an epidural. I had been expecting a pat on the back, maybe an extra helping of chocolate pudding on my dinner tray. Instead, they told me our baby was broken. Before the end of Lizzie's first night on this planet, it was made clear to us that her condition would require multiple surgeries, consults with an array of specialists, and perhaps a lifetime of speech and language challenges.

We left the hospital the next day with a list of phone numbers. Apparently, there were whole medical teams dedicated to children born with cleft palates. But it was Saturday, and no one would be in the office until next week. So we planned to hunker down, feed our baby, and try to get some sleep. Surely, if they had sent us home, setting up Lizzie's specialized care could wait the weekend.

That evening, Lizzie was lethargic. She would nurse for only a few minutes and then fall asleep. I thought it was a little odd, but I figured childbirth had been exhausting for both of us. When she went back to sleep, so did I. On her first night home, we both slept through the night.

Remembering how miserably baby Katie had slept, I was delighted to have my easy baby, my good sleeper.

The next morning, we continued this strange dance. I woke Lizzie up to nurse, she latched for a few seconds, and then she drifted back to sleep. I read a short blurb about cleft babies in *The Womanly Art of Breastfeeding*, which emphasized the difficulties of feeding babies with cleft palates. I don't remember everything it said, only that it was opposite a chapter entitled "When Your Baby Dies." Midday, we called the doctor.

God bless Lizzie's pediatrician, Dr. Dorfman, who met us in her office on a Sunday afternoon. Lizzie had been a whopping eight pounds, fourteen ounces at birth (when I am pregnant, I eat a lot of cake). Three days later, she was just shy of seven pounds.

"If we can't get this baby to eat, I'm going to need to readmit her to the hospital and intubate her," the doctor counseled. She was gentle but firm. She sat with us for hours, on her day off, through two sleepy feeding cycles. We took off Lizzie's clothes, blew on her belly, even rubbed water on her feet. As soon as she was awake, we put her back on my breast.

I don't like to talk about breastfeeding. I know it is natural and beautiful and everything, but nobody really wants to hear about it. In this case, though, a few details are necessary. A woman's body makes enough milk to feed her baby, but the baby has to cue the milk. When a baby suckles, the milk *lets down*. The child initially gets the watery foremilk and then, with continued suckling, the hindmilk. It is this fatty hindmilk that helps the baby gain weight. Because of the U-shaped hole in the roof of Lizzie's mouth, and because of her tiny tongue, she could never create any suction. I had nursed a baby before, so my body was ready. I had foremilk leaking everywhere. Enough to feed a litter of stray kittens, had I encountered one. Lizzie had caught some of this early milk but never pulled down any nutrient-dense hindmilk on her own. In the couple of days that she had been alive, she had never actually been nursing, only attempting to nurse, as her instinct told her to, and she had utterly exhausted herself in the process. As the cool-guy resident had mentioned, the craniofacial liaison was away when Lizzie was born. What he had failed to consider was that meant we would slip through the cracks at the hospital without ever being fully counseled about how difficult it was going to be to feed this child.

Over the next week, we saw another pediatrician, a nurse practitioner, a lactation consultant, and several members of the craniofacial department at a nearby medical center. We were given special bottles and nipples, pep talks, and formula. Everyone had different advice for getting milk into Lizzie. But they all agreed on one thing: she would never be able to breastfeed.

This news devastated me. And my heartbreak surprised me. With Katie, I had not taken to nursing with ease or grace. While my mom friends wanted to sit in coffee shops and openly nurse their babies, I much preferred to cover up. I had skinny-dipped in college, but when it came to feeding a baby, I was modest. I was also resentful of the time and strain on my body. I felt tethered. I had read enough pamphlets and posters while waiting in my OB/GYN's office to know that breastfeeding was better for a baby's brain development, but I was pretty sure that breastfeeding was detrimental to a mother's whole person. I was tired all the time. I subsisted on cereal and candy. And then I cried when my pants didn't fit. No, I had not loved breastfeeding. So one would think that being told I could not nurse Lizzie would have been an unburdening. A chance to give up a practice that had often made me feel like a prisoner in my own body.

Instead, being unable to breastfeed Lizzie was yet another thing to mourn. Yet another way that I was failing this child. I had already botched her development inside of my womb, and now I had lost the ability to nourish and sustain her outside of my body. I was overcome with grief.

Every Two to Three Hours

My pregnancy with Lizzie had been a normal one—I took my prenatal vitamins and kept my doctors' appointments and did not eat raw fish or soft cheese. But I have always figured that there must have been something I did wrong. I climbed on a chair a couple of times to swap out posters on my classroom bulletin board. I took cold medicine one night when I could not sleep. I did not always eat as many fruits and vegetables as I should have. Did I walk too little? Should I have done more yoga? I know now that there is no use in this line of questioning. But during the weeks and months after Lizzie's birth, I continued to interrogate myself. *What did I do?* This child should have grown and flourished inside my body. I was in complete control of what nourishment she received and what comfort she experienced. Whatever it was that happened to her in there, whatever combination of stimuli that caused her chin to tuck and her tongue to raise and the roof of her mouth to fail to form completely, whatever it was, it was my fault. I felt like it was my duty to heal her. Breastmilk, expressed and offered to her from a bottle, felt like the only gift I had to give.

Lizzie's pediatrician arranged for the maternity ward to loan us a pump. It was a hospital-grade monstrosity that seemed better suited to livestock than humans. I sat at our tiny kitchen table with a glass of water, a how-to essay, and a canister of baby formula. I attached these ridiculous sucking shuttle cups to my breasts and turned the machine on. It tugged and whirred, but otherwise, nothing happened. Cuddling a baby, nursing a baby, that made sense. There was an emotional connection. My body made milk without me having to think about it. But this? How could I convince the milk to flow out of me and into a plastic cup? Was I supposed to bond with my breast pump? I managed to collect maybe a quarter of an ounce. Not even close to what the doctor said Lizzie needed for each feeding.

Ken looked at the tiny amount of liquid. "Is this all?" he asked.

"Yup," I replied. "If Lizzie finishes that before I produce any more, I will open this canister and mix the formula myself."

I drank three glasses of water, sat down with my stupid pump, and tried again. I still felt bovine. But I refused to let that deter me. One of the websites I consulted said to picture waterfalls. I pictured waterfalls. Another said to visualize the face of my infant. I closed my eyes and thought of Lizzie, of her dark blue eyes and her tiny rosebud mouth. After fifteen minutes, I had collected maybe half an ounce more of this yellowish milk—"liquid gold," one of the nurses had called it—and Lizzie had fallen asleep to the whir, whir, whir of the machine without even drinking the first quarter ounce. I capped the bottle and slid it into the fridge. Then I set my alarm clock to wake up in two hours and try again. All through that night, Ken and I both awoke every few hours. I sat and pumped. And he tried to feed whatever I produced to our tiny baby girl.

Of course, looking back, I realize that I did not need to put myself through any of that. Despite how it is often presented, formula and breastmilk are not mutually exclusive. Rather than wreck ourselves try-ing to pump and feed all night, Ken and I could have reserved formula for night feedings and offered Lizzie breastmilk throughout the day. We could have easily given Lizzie both. But at the time, we were both swept up in the urgency and the uncertainty of what life was going to be like for this child. We had a visceral need to try to make whatever we could right for Lizzie. We could not take it easy when we knew her path was going to be so difficult.

The next few weeks were a blur, a constant struggle to nourish and strengthen our baby. We were counseled to try a half dozen different cleft bottles, a shot glass, an eyedropper, and even our fingertips to attempt to feed Lizzie. We settled on a nipple from Japan, but we had no translation of the instructions, so each session was an act of frustration and illusion. When we tipped the bottle toward Lizzie's mouth, it looked like she was taking in milk. But when we set it down on the table to see what she had eaten, the measure was the same.

In the end, Dr. Dorfman did not need to intubate. Instead, we woke Lizzie every two to three hours, day and night, and eased milk into her, drop by magical drop. We learned what angle worked best for feeding her. How to hold the bottle just right. How to prop her up to avoid milk sloshing up through the large hole in her palate and coming out her nose. How to tell the difference between when she was just gumming the nipple and when she was actually swallowing milk. Unless we were driving to a medical test or surgical consult, Ken and I were seldom awake at the same time. If we could just grow her big enough, the doctors assured us, then they could begin stitching up her mouth, which, in time, would make it easier for Lizzie to eat, breathe, and, hopefully, eventually, to speak.

And then we moved away.

This may sound crazy. After all, we had just spent the first few weeks of our baby's life trying to grow and stabilize her. Now we were leaving town?

Though in retrospect it sounds bonkers, even to us, it was not a spur-of-the-moment decision. We'd planned the move months before. Ken was finished with law school. I had earned my master's degree. I had a teaching job that I loved, and he had several big career opportunities in the works, but we knew we might never have another chance to take this kind of time together again, to pause for a bit and just be a family. In the months before Lizzie was born, we found an off-season vacation rental in Virginia for a fraction of our mortgage payment in Connecticut. We rented out our New Haven house, I applied for a childcare leave of absence from my job, and we planned a holiday by the sea. We would fish and swim and walk along the shore. We would drink tea and write while our kids napped. With some scrimping, we figured we had enough saved for five or six months.

Of course, the moment Lizzie was born, our plan seemed foolhardy. We could not live in some off-season backwater town, twenty minutes from the nearest grocery store and almost an hour from a hospital. We needed access to first-rate medical care and baked goods. This was hardly the time for a vacation.

But Connecticut was an expensive place to live. We had no house—our tenants had already moved in before Lizzie was born. We had been staying in a friend's empty place while she was away for the summer. We had no jobs—I could not conceive of going back to teaching while Lizzie was so fragile. Ken had stalled and put off interviews for our family sabbatical. Even if he renewed those conversations, it would be another month at least before he found a placement, and there was no telling where that job would be. He was interviewing all over the country. We knew that, together, we could weather any storm. We just needed to find some place cheap to weather it.

So we went.

Colonial Beach, Virginia

In September, when Lizzie was five weeks old, the doctors declared us free to go. Lizzie was back up to her birth weight—the standard of care, apparently, in cases like ours. And as long as we got her in to see a pediatrician as soon as we arrived in Virginia, there was no real harm in going. Her first procedure would not be scheduled until she was six months old. We would be two hours from Washington, DC, and had a referral to a surgeon there. So we packed up our used minivan—a car I swore I'd never drive—and headed south. We got caught in traffic in New York City and stopped to visit friends in Maryland. In keeping with our travel history, the six-hour drive took us two and a half days.

We had thought the quiet location might be idyllic—and it was. There were sunrises over the water and birds flying low along the deserted shore. But we did not know that it would also be the most difficult months of our marriage.

We arrived on Labor Day weekend. Our two-bedroom cottage backed right up to the bay. We could smell barbecues in adjacent yards and see boats pulling inner tubes out on the Chesapeake. Everywhere we looked, there was an end-of-summer party. Nobody paid us any mind. We cooked three hamburgers on the stove—we'd left our grill in Connecticut—watched a *Project Runway* rerun, and went to bed.

Most infants wake in the night crying for Mom or Dad. Parents learn to loathe those middle-of-the-night whimpers that signify another bleary-eyed feeding. But for the first three months of her life, Lizzie never woke us up. If we did not rouse her, she would simply sleep through the night. With Katie, we had been desperate for rest. With Lizzie, we had to set our alarm and wake her up. We had to keep her growing.

When Katie was our only child, I never understood that expression about throwing a kid out of the nest. But she was four years old now, and she did not need me as much as her little sister did. It was tempting to plop Katie in front of a video so I could give my full attention to Lizzie. And some days, I did that. Other days, I set up Katie's easel on the back porch, and she would paint picture after picture. Looking back, I think it was probably some self-assigned art therapy. This little girl had left her preschool, her home, and her friends to come live by the bay with distracted parents and a sister she quickly came to resent. One Sunday after church, Katie told me, "Wouldn't it be fun if we put baby Lizzie in a basket?"

"Sure . . ." I said, warily.

"Then we could float her out to sea," said Katie, "like Moses."

I had read that it was natural for older children to say things like "I hate the baby" or "I wish we could give the baby back to the hospital." But I had not been prepared for Katie to make Biblical justifications for ridding us of her little sister.

We had chosen not to enroll Katie in preschool. Those we had considered were too expensive or too far away. One of our neighbors drove his children over an hour each way. But I did not want Katie to be lonely, so I did my best to find her some semblance of a community. We discovered a small library about twenty minutes away. There was no story time or children's room, and it was only open a few days a week, but it was a destination. Sometimes it took us an hour or two to get into the car—between feeding and pooping and changing and pumping—and a couple of hours to repeat that process while we were there. But it was somewhere to go.

After almost a month in Virginia, we also discovered a YWCA only half an hour in the other direction. The caregivers at the Y were Lizzie's first babysitters. They never kept her for long, just enough time for me to hop in the pool with my Katie. To splash and play tag and carry her effortlessly in my arms and try to convince her that even though everything felt crazy and different, it was still very much the same, and that even though there were two children now, somehow my heart still had more than enough room for her.

Though we lived with the Chesapeake in our backyard, I only swam outside with Katie a handful of times. Fall came quickly that year. The water grew cool and the air crisp. On one of our chilly dips, I spotted a family well down the shore. This was a first. After Labor Day, the whole area had cleared out. Vacationers packed up their chairs. Most of the nearby houses closed up as well. So when I spotted that family, Katie and I all but sprinted down the beach to meet them. As we got closer, I grew self-conscious. Wouldn't it seem desperate to barge into them like that? I convinced myself that it would look way more natural if we kind of "accidentally" washed up out of the bay. So Katie and I treaded back into the water, waded down shore, and then tumbled awkwardly onto the dirty brown sand.

Right from the start, the parents and I had almost nothing in common. They were drinking Diet Mountain Dew, listening to AM talk radio, and sunbathing in October. They had worn tennis shoes rather than flip-flops down to the sand. Dad was keen on day-trading, and Mom worked in podiatry. But Katie and their son and daughter began splashing and laughing, and I made it my new goal in life to engage these folks as long as they'd tolerate me. We talked tech stocks and bunions as the sun waned, and I learned that they lived only a mile or so away. Before the afternoon was over, I had asked them for dinner the next week and they had invited us to a baptism the following morning. It seemed one of the children was being saved. I woke up the next day too ragtag from a night of Lizzie-ing to attend, but Ken dutifully transported Katie to the Pentecostal church at nine o'clock to witness the baptism of a child he did not know and share a luncheon with a family he had never met. My husband is a good man.

In the four months we spent in Virginia, Luke and Isabella were the only friends Katie ever made. Their parents' religious and political convictions were different than mine, and I never did get a handle on day-trading, but that didn't matter; they opened their home to us during a difficult time. We shared stories about marriage and in-laws and homework and carpooling, and their children made Katie feel normal. For that, I am forever grateful.

That December, a blizzard later named "Snowpocalypse" dumped nearly two feet of snow on Washington, DC, and left the city and the surrounding areas immobilized for several days. We had not thought to pack snow gear for our beach trip. I put Katie in three pairs of pants, zipped Lizzie up in my coat, and tromped out into the winter wonderland beside the sea. As I looked at our surroundings, it was as though Virginia itself echoed our family confusion. Were we coming or going? Pulling ourselves together or falling apart? Should we settle

Right from the start, the parents and I had almost nothing in common. But Katie and their son and daughter began splashing and laughing, and I made it my new goal in life to engage these folks as long as they'd tolerate me.

5 TALK TO STRANGERS

We stopped steering, stopped plotting our course, stopped planning for the future, and simply held onto one another while we waited for the winds to blow themselves out.

 **Every Storm Ends**

into a life here or beat feet back to civilization?

Looking back, I am thankful for those first precious moments in the hospital with Lizzie when I naively thought everything was fine. I clung to the hope that one day, all would be right again. The snow lasted through Christmas, but eventually the last of it melted. Not long after, our family's storm subsided as well. In the meantime, there was nothing Ken and I could do but hunker down. We stopped steering, stopped plotting our course, stopped planning for the future, and simply held on to one another while we waited for the winds to blow themselves out.

6: Sailing to Lunch

In the nearly twenty years that we have been together, Annmarie and I have spent our share of time apart. From her time at camp to my Navy deployments to Afghanistan, we managed to keep our sense of togetherness intact. But never had we felt more distant than when we lived in the same tiny cottage on the banks of the Chesapeake.

Those were the dark days of our marriage. Before Lizzie's birth, we had looked forward to this sabbatical. In our heads, it sounded perfect—a place to watch sunsets and learn to be a family of four, a space to finally write our books as we subsisted on our meager savings. But the brutal realities of nursing Lizzie to health forced us into survival mode. Annmarie and I devoted ourselves entirely to the kids. Her primary focus was getting enough food into Lizzie to make her well, while my attention was split between Lizzie's midnight feedings and providing Katie with enough love and time to reassure her everything would be all right.

This left Annmarie and I with absolutely nothing in reserve for each other. For the four months we spent holed up in that cabin, we were almost never awake at the same time. Lizzie's round-the-clock care schedule meant that when one of us was feeding her, the other had to rest. As husband and wife, we had precious few moments alone. The only break I can remember was when my parents visited for a few days to help us out. Grandma H stood midnight shifts with Lizzie while Grandpa H owned the kitchen. But it was too brief of a reprieve. When they left, Annmarie and I were back to our grueling routine. Of the two of us, she had the worst of it. She did not change her socks. She had little time to talk to strangers.

In our wildest dreams, we never imagined it would be so hard. Even after we knew Lizzie would need constant care, Annmarie and I thought our sabbatical-turned-convalescence might offer some much-needed downtime. What we did not anticipate was Katie's reaction to this family upheaval. The first weeks at our beach cottage, she seemed to be handling things well enough. With her easel set up on the back porch, she would gaze out over the water and paint for hours on end. Annmarie and I paid scant attention. I was glad Katie found some way to occupy her time while we devoted ourselves to her little sister. Shame on us for not realizing sooner how unhappy our little girl was.

It took Annmarie, as exhausted as she was, to finally listen—or, rather, *see*. Katie's paintings had no joy in them. There were no smiling stick-figure parents, no bright orange sunsets over the ocean, no birthday cakes. Instead, Katie's paintings showed a family coming apart. Mom holding a baby, crying, while Dad slept. Cakes with no candles. Black and blue sunsets.

"She needs you," Annmarie said.

As close as Katie was to us, she felt alone. So, the next morning, I embarked on a quest, determined to turn our four-month banishment into some kind of adventure.

Not far down the beach from our cottage stood a copse of scrubby trees. Buried in the undergrowth was a sailboat, weathered and beaten, just big enough for a crew of two. We asked the neighbors about it. It had lain there for years, left by a previous homeowner who never returned. We dragged it free, scrubbed it down, patched the sail, and, with a couple five-dollar tubes of caulk, resealed (sort of) the hull. For a full week, Katie and I spent our daylight hours at the water's edge putting our tiny craft back together. It might not have looked like much to anyone else, but Katie and I adored that boat.

"What do we call it?" she asked.

"How about . . . 'Fawkes,'" I said. We were reading *Harry Potter* together—Fawkes was a phoenix that belonged to the head wizard. I explained the symbolism. "You know, Fawkes, like the bird in *Chamber of Secrets*? The one that looks all ragged and beat-up but is brought back to life just when it's needed most?"

Katie made a face. "Nah," she said. "Let's call it 'Marlon.'"

"Really?" I said. "'Marlon?'"

"Yeah," she said. "It's a good name for a boat."

"Okay . . . 'Marlon' it is."

With a can of spray paint, we scrawled *Marlon* in bright pink letters on the stern. Years later, in an offhand conversation with Katie while watching a rerun of *Finding Nemo*, I learned that she had not named our boat *Marlon* but *Marlin* after Nemo's dad. The name fit: cartoon clownfish and human dad, both in search of a kid we thought we'd lost.

From the moment Katie and I christened our little sailboat, the bayhead became our playground. Where the muddy brown water of the Potomac ran into the Chesapeake, we became explorers, adventurers—buccaneers. To her everlasting credit, Annmarie battened the hatches, doubled down with Lizzie, and gave me the time I needed to devote to Katie.

Katie and I *did* talk to strangers. In our neck of the woods, there were some real characters. We met a crab fisherman, old and grizzled, who spent his mornings on the water hauling in traps and his afternoons tending a massive aluminum kettle, four feet deep and as many across. It was so heavy that lifting it required the aid of a makeshift crane. Katie loved dropping by in the early evening when the giant batches of Maryland blue crab were done cooking and ready to be tipped. A small crane hoisted the pot off the propane burner, and with one mighty heave of a rope attached to the rim, a thousand steaming red crabs came pouring over the sorting table. Katie jumped up and down and ran up to pick out the biggest ones.

I don't think our fisherman friend ever had such an enthusiastic customer; he went out of his way to make Katie feel special. He gave us two traps to set off our own beach and advice on how to rig them.

"Make sure you bait 'em every morning," he said. "Crabbies know when you're bein' cheap."

I taught Katie to use a cast net, and when the tide rolled in, we stalked the shallows looking for schools of baitfish. With a little practice, we became experts. A few well-aimed throws, and our bait buckets were full.

Most mornings, we set out early. First stop was our traps. We emptied the night's haul and reset them with freshly cut bait. Then, with me as first mate, Katie captained *Marlon* for the day's voyage, always exploring some new section of coastline. We packed a dry bag with extra clothes, dried fruit, Ramen noodles, a tin pot, and a lighter. When we got hungry, we found a beach to build a campfire and make a meal. Katie reveled in the adventure of it. There was something more, though. With her little boat and crab traps, Katie now had a way to feel like an important part of Team Harbaugh. She had a purpose.

"We're feeding the family, Daddy!" she often said as we hauled in our traps.

The Harbaughs had plenty of food, of course. We weren't that poor. But almost everything we caught we turned into a meal. Blue crabs were always a hit. Catfish less so. Every once in a while, we'd get lucky. Pulling our boat up to the milk-jug float, Katie would heave on the line. As soon as the trap lifted off the bottom, she knew she had something big. The rope would quiver, then jerk, as whatever was stuck made a desperate attempt to escape. Somehow, every few weeks, one of the giant rockfish that cruised the muddy shallows of the Chesapeake would wriggle its way into our trap. They may have been dumb, even for fish, but they sure were tasty.

At the tender age of four, Katie learned how to gut and scale and how to build a fire on the sand. We rigged a spit to turn the big fish, and, as the sun dipped low, we brought sweet potatoes wrapped in foil down from the house. When everything was done, we ate with our fingers like *wild things*. And as the fire died, we stared at its glowing embers and plotted the next day. Sometimes, Annmarie roused herself and carried Lizzie down, swaddled tightly against the evening chill. Those were magical moments: the whole family gathered to share a feast that Katie and I had pulled from the water. I was always exhausted, but I knew that these adventures would last forever in Katie's memory of Colonial Beach.

Soft Shells

At first glance, *Callinectes sapidus* is a weird creature to behold. It walks, or rather skitters, sideways. Its eyes protrude on stalks, and its face is armored and spiny with mandibles that open up like something out of a horror film. The Maryland blue crab has been compared to the alien from the *Predator* movies. It is similarly bad tempered, and if it could launch laser-guided missiles at its enemies, it probably would. Still, this ornery crustacean is a staple of daily life around the Chesapeake, and Katie and I became the little beast's biggest fans.

As she did her part to take care of the family, Katie gained confidence in small ways—like learning to pick up crabs with her bare hands. The real trick, she discovered, is knowing where to grab them. Their pincers are fierce, and a big one can squeeze hard enough to draw blood. But they have a weakness. An Achilles leg, if you will. Their very last appendage is a swimming paddle, and, crucially, its topmost joint is out of reach of the claws. Grab it there, between forefinger and thumb, and you won't get pinched.

Katie loved showing off. After hauling in the traps and loosening the wire holding down the door, we dumped them over *Marlon's* deck. Sometimes one or two came flopping out; occasionally, a whole dozen.

As they scampered wildly, Katie reached down and grabbed each by its rear leg, depositing them in her bucket to thrash about. That was how most crabs behaved. But once in a hundred times, we came across an anomaly. A crab that would flop onto the deck and lay there. No flailing, no claws raised in a defensive stance. When Katie went to grab one of these, they did not react. They simply hung limp. Not dead—we could tell because their eye stalks still moved—but utterly unable to protect themselves.

"Daddy, it's *soft*," Katie said the first time she held one of them up.

"I know what this is," I said. "It's a soft-shell crab."

"A what?" Katie said.

"A soft-shell crab," I said. "Every crab, every crustacean, actually, needs to leave its shell if it wants to get bigger. It's called molting."

"So, it needs to leave its shell to grow?" Katie asked.

"Yep," I said.

"But . . . that's its *home*," she said. "It doesn't seem fair."

Katie and I held the crab in our hands, turning it over, feeling its paper-thin skin. I told her about exoskeletons, how they didn't grow with their animals like our internal skeletons did. If they had any chance of getting bigger and stronger, of becoming more able to survive and have little crab babies of their own, they needed to leave their old shells and grow newer, roomier ones. They would find a safe place away from predators and begin the slow process of extracting their soft bodies. Then they would swell up and fill out their new skin. In time, their papery shell would harden into armor. For young blue crabs, this might happen every few weeks. For the big ones, years could pass between molts. But for young and old alike, there is a critical, life-threatening window of vulnerability. When the old shell is abandoned and the new one is still wrinkled and expanding, the crab is at its weakest. Most stay holed up, buried under mud or hidden in a crevasse. Every so often, though, one might stray, tempted by a ball of freshly cut bait in a trap set by a little girl and her dad. And then Katie would be turning a soft-shell crab in her palm, marveling at the wondrous complexity of the world around her.

"Should we put it back?" I asked. Seeing the helpless creature in Katie's hands, I saw our own family. The Harbaughs, holed up, waiting for a safe moment to reemerge, for our shells to grow back stronger.

"You mean, so it can grow its shell back?" Katie said.

"Yeah, you know, let nature take its proper course," I said. "Let this crab get bigger."

"Um, Dad, I think nature has taken its course," Katie said. "This crab crawled into my pot. So now I'm gonna eat it."

So much for sentiment.

To this day, fresh-caught soft-shell crabs are my favorite thing in the world to eat. Sautéed in butter and garlic, they have just the right crunch and that perfect balance of salty and sweet. A perfectly cooked soft shell (pan-fried, not battered, and fresh, NEVER frozen) brings back every good memory of those months on the Chesapeake with Katie and the knowledge that, given a little time and shelter, even the most vulnerable creatures can eventually flourish again.

SAILING TO LUNCH

Patrolling the waters off Colonial Beach, setting our traps day after day, Katie turned into quite the sailor. For a not-quite-five-year-old, she was brave, and she had an intuitive feel for how a sailboat should move through the water. My coaching technique may have been unorthodox, but it worked. As soon we pushed off the shore and had enough depth to set the dagger board, I threw a line off the stern and hopped in the water. Katie handled the sail and steered, and I dragged behind, shouting commands.

"Haul in the sheet . . . you're luffing . . . bear off!"

Katie kept one hand on the tiller to guide *Marlon* and another on the rope that controlled the sail. She was a quick study and, before long, had it figured out. It was like her arms did the thinking for her. She learned how much sail to let out or haul in, how close to the wind she could point, and how to take a wave head on. I was perfectly content as her sea anchor, dragging behind, marveling at the way this little girl handled a boat all by herself.

In heavy seas, of course, I took charge. Even in the sheltered Chesapeake, the waves could stand up. Certainly big enough to swamp, or even capsize, a tiny boat such as ours. Weather sometimes rolled in with little warning. One afternoon after setting our traps, a storm caught us off guard. I had seen the black line of clouds in the distance and guessed it would miss us by a safe margin. But the wind shifted and caught us out. I took the tiller and sheet from Katie and made for the shoreline. There was no lightning, but we could not beat the rain. The sky opened up, and the sea leapt around us. Katie wrapped her arms around the mast, and every time we plowed through a wave, she whooped with delight. We were drenched but making good progress. Then, out of nowhere, two waves broke in quick succession over the bow. The first hit Katie full on, loosening her grip on the mast. The second washed her overboard.

For a split second, I panicked. One moment, she was there; the next, she was gone. Then I reacted. I had practiced man-overboard drills a thousand times, from family sailing trips as a kid to my honeymoon with Annmarie to coaching sailing at The Citadel. Now, that muscle memory kicked in. I turned the boat, let out the sail, and scanned the water. I could not see Katie anywhere. Her bright pink life jacket should have been clearly visible and not far in front of me. But she wasn't there.

Then, behind me, a whoop.

I turned. Katie was holding tight to the rope trailing off the stern, the one I used to drag behind the boat.

"Daddy, that was *fun!*" she cried. "Can we do it again?"

I pulled her in, regained my composure, and sat her in the cockpit with one arm wrapped tightly around her waist.

"Here, you take the sail; I'll steer," I said. "And try to stay aboard this time."

For Katie, this was one of the biggest lessons from our time in Colonial Beach: adventures are worth the mishaps. So long as we were prepared (as in, wearing our life jackets), getting washed overboard was not the worst thing that could happen to a little girl. Far more dangerous would be never setting out in the first place, never learning how to measure risk, never having to face—and overcome—one's fears.

That was the only time I ever lost Katie, however briefly, to the sea. As a rule, we gave thanks every time the Chesapeake offered up her gifts, whether a trap bursting with crabs or a long cruise to a distant beach.

We weren't always so bold. Some days, we turned downright lazy. We slept in and set out late. No cast netting in the shallows, no buckets of baitfish for the traps. We told each other the crabs needed another day to soak, but really, we just wanted to treat ourselves. So we ignored our chores, put off adventure for another day, and made for a little seafood restaurant across the inlet.

> *Getting washed overboard was not the worst thing that could happen to a little girl. Far more dangerous would be never setting out in the first place.*
>
> **I   ADVENTURES ARE WORTH THE MISHAPS**

It felt good to let someone else take care of us. Even if it was only for one meal. On those days, Katie and I would sit quietly and let the food come. We were warm and dry and content in our idleness. Lunch, done like that, could take hours. Eventually, we would notice the sun beginning to cast longer shadows, and we'd head back to the boat. With our lazy tanks at full capacity, we'd pile back into *Marlon* and head for home.

As thrilling as these adventures were, after four months, Annmarie's and my savings ran out. We began living off credit cards. Worse still, our health insurance was about to expire. We had scheduled a surgery for Lizzie with no way to pay for it. One of us needed to get a job. I had made several contacts back in law school and had anticipated working for the federal government. But those jobs were slow in coming. I even talked to a military recruiter to see if they would let me back in. While in the early stages of interviews, a consulting firm contacted me out of the blue on the recommendation of a friend.

It was not my dream job. But at that point, what the Harbaughs needed was a way to pay medical bills and make sure Lizzie had the best doctors money could buy. So I took the gig, my first desk job, consulting with a firm based out of Cleveland. When we packed up our belongings, we left the boat and crab traps behind. The stories they'd brought us were one of a kind, and I knew it would be a mistake to try to re-create them on Lake Erie. More importantly, our shells had finally hardened. The Harbaughs were ready to reemerge. Lizzie was growing, Annmarie was coming back up for air, and my brave Katie saw the world as a place where adventure could happen—where she could master her fear and provide for her family from a little boat named *Marlon*.

Looking back, it is clearer than ever how deeply unfair all of this was to my wife. She never once set foot in that boat. She never had the energy or the time. Annmarie pumped all Lizzie's milk, measured and recorded the ounces for every feeding, and ensured she woke up. Sometimes, it took a whole hour just to get those few drops of sustenance into Lizzie. To this day, I feel guilty for not shouldering more of that burden. And Annmarie mourns the months she was not able to be a better mother to our oldest daughter. But then I look at our girls. Whatever we did worked. Lizzie came through that storm strong—the kind of kid who skins her knee and gets right back up. And Katie learned to be an explorer—a child fearless in the water, a sailor, a swimmer, and a lover of seafood to boot. Even during this difficult time, those adventures with Katie were free.

Even during this difficult time, those adventures with Katie were free.

3 Happiness is Cheap

7: VITAL SIGNS AND A NEW NORMAL

I t took nearly six months, but we finally found a kind of equilibrium. Thanks to that special cleft palate bottle we ordered from Japan, Lizzie gained weight. Slowly, at first, and then steadily. Ken took the consulting job in Ohio, and we relocated to a tiny village outside Cleveland to be near my family. The town was called Chagrin Falls, and living there was like stepping into a postcard. In addition to the picturesque waterfalls, we had an old-fashioned hardware store, a sheriff who eschewed parking tickets in favor of friendly warnings, and a shop devoted entirely to selling candy and popcorn. It was a modern-day Mayberry.

We enrolled Katie in preschool, and she flourished. I think a part of her missed those days of sailing and adventuring with her dad, but she was also delighted to be back amongst children her own age. At her eco-hip Precious Resources Preschool, she practiced yoga, composting, owl-pellet dissection, endangered species preservation, and how to paint like Matisse. Ken's job had him on the road Monday through Friday, so Katie's sublime teacher, Ms. Barbara, became a trusted member of my parenting team.

Though only weeks into his new job, Ken was granted time off for Lizzie's first big operation. We left Katie with my parents and drove the winding Pennsylvania turnpike to Washington, DC. Though we no longer lived in the area, we had forged a relationship with the craniofacial team down there. After multiple consultations and tough questions, we came to trust the surgeons and their plans for our little girl. The night before the surgery, we arrived at our hotel near the children's hospital and ducked into an adjacent restaurant for dinner. It was surprisingly crowded for a Sunday night. "It's always like this," our server explained. "But especially on February 14th."

It was Valentine's Day. Neither Ken nor I had remembered. We did not exchange cards or chocolates but grasped hands, gazed at Lizzie, and prayed that everything would be all right in the morning.

The hospital scheduled the youngest children for the earliest surgeries, so we reported for intake at 6:00 a.m. Because Lizzie would be anesthetized, we had not fed her since midnight. I distracted her with a stuffed elephant and a board book while Ken completed paperwork and verified the new insurance numbers. Then we entered a series of waiting rooms. Someone tried to take vital signs, but when it came to measuring Lizzie's blood pressure, even the smallest cuff was still too big. It kept sliding off of her arm. Someone else brought us a plastic bag for Lizzie's clothes. We changed her into the tiniest hospital gown I had ever seen. It was robin's-egg blue and cottony soft. Lizzie looked adorable in her baby scrubs. Conversely, Ken and I were issued an enormous jumpsuit, a scratchy one-size-fits-all disposable thing, with lemon-yellow booties and an elastic shower cap to match. Though it seemed like several yards of material, the ensemble was intended for only one person.

"One parent is permitted to escort the child into the operating room," said our firm but friendly surgical liaison. We had been informed of this ahead of time but had hoped that when the day came, we would both be able to weasel our way back there. Ken and I were good at that sort of thing. We were the kind of folks who landed tickets to sold-out shows and found the last parking spot in the supposedly full lot. We once snuck an entire pizza into a movie theater. We made our own luck. But not here.

In the hospital at 6:23 in the morning, we had to choose. It was a little like one of those '70s after-school specials when a child of divorced parents has to decide to live with either Mom or Dad. *Who do I love more?* It was all well and good to believe that everyone loved everyone equally and all the same—until you had a single hospital gown in your hand.

Ken and I both loved Lizzie to the moon and back, but only one of us could make the trip. Only one of us would hold and comfort our daughter in the moments before she fell asleep. I hesitated briefly, but we both knew the answer: it had to be me. I had logged more hours with this sickly baby than anyone. I had pumped milk for her until my nipples bled, foregone sleep and self-care, and held her night after night watching infomercials for vacuum cleaners and fitness programs. Mine was the face she needed to see as she lost consciousness. I slid the jumpsuit over my yoga pants and stepped into the elastic slippers like a pair of indoor galoshes. Ken fastened the back of the gown over my hoodie. I was ready.

Unlike the medical professionals I had seen on TV, I looked neither sexy nor dramatic. In my circus tent of an ensemble, I felt like a bad school mascot or a rejected Teletubby. But this costume helped me distance myself from the difficult business at hand. As Annmarie, mother of two, I might have broken down. But as Annmarie, Lemon-Yellow Care Bear, I had a role to play. It was my job to comfort and bounce and sing my baby all the way to the operating room. My hairnet was my helmet.

Lizzie was six months and two days old. There was no way for me to explain to her what was about to happen: that doctors were going to peel away skin from the inside of her mouth and throat and weave it into a makeshift palate; that they would stitch it together where the roof of her mouth should have been; that a single string would be sewn to the center of her tongue, where it would hang out of her mouth, so if the swelling became too great and her breathing was cut off, they would have a way to quickly open the airway; that another doctor would insert tubes in her ears; that she would be anesthetized, her breathing controlled by a technician and a machine; that we would not be with her. We had never not been with her. That was the rule with Lizzie. She needed us the most. She slept in our bedroom. She drowsed in our arms. There was no way for me to prepare Lizzie for this. And there was no way for me to prepare myself. We just had to do it.

The OR nurse called Lizzie's name. I held my baby girl in her tiny blue scrubs and walked her down a white hallway as I sang "Twinkle, Twinkle, Little Star."

Ours was a relatively moderate procedure. This was not an emergency. The surgeons were hopeful about rates of success. And yet, holding my child, looking into her eyes as they fluttered shut, and feeling her small body go slack on the operating table was one of the most difficult things I have ever done. I have never been able to shake the feeling of that room. The bright lights. The stainless steel. The sterile instruments. And me staggering back into the hallway, choking on the fear I had swallowed so Lizzie would not see it.

If you ever have the occasion to sit in a pediatric surgical waiting room, you will learn it is not a great place for crafting. When faced with a wait of several hours, some people optimistically bring projects—scrapbooks, photo albums, recipes to compile. But no one makes a dent. No one is knitting or completing a Sudoku book, though some folks sit with pencils, needles, and yarn. A hospital waiting room is an okay place to catch up on Candy Crush or to watch whatever vapid rerun is showing on Nickelodeon. And it is an excellent place to pray. It does not matter your color, class, or creed; when it comes to waiting for doctors to finish operating on a child, everyone is praying. They are holding Bibles and clutching Kleenex. They are weeping quietly or staring sternly into space. A few even make small talk near the vending machines. But no matter what they are doing or not doing, everyone is uttering the same plea: "Let this child be okay." We waited for hours, and I prayed those words again and again. *Lord, let this child be okay. Dear God, let this child be okay.*

And then a green number appeared on a computer screen indicating that Lizzie had been moved to recovery. Soon after, the doctors appeared to describe what they had done and what to expect for the next few days.

The ENT, Dr. Gurian, suggested we carry Lizzie's antibiotic ear drops in our pockets to warm them up before we administered them. "It's the cold that bothers babies most of all," he said. And Dr. Baker reminded us to stay ahead of Lizzie's pain.

There is no ritual, no bread-and-butter gift that fits the circumstance when a surgeon safely delivers your child back to you. But there should be. If I had had an extra ruby, I would have gladly handed it over. If I was a person who played the lottery, I would have given either one of them my winning ticket. These days, we bring Lizzie's clinicians cookies or homemade bread when we go in for her yearly consults. But our hands were empty that February. We had only thought about the moments up to and including the surgery. Neither Ken nor I had thought much about what would happen afterwards. One of the doctors stuck out a hand to shake, and I awkwardly went in for a hug instead, resulting in a stiff jab to my ribs when he maintained the handshake position.

RECOVERY 1

Just as mine was the last face Lizzie gazed upon as she went under, I was determined that I would be there when she awoke. Lizzie's breathing in the recovery room was percussive. She took strange, staggered breaths as though she had just finished a workout. And she whimpered. I thought I had heard all of her cries by then—the ones that told me she was hungry or tired or wet. But I had never heard her cry in pain. Her face was swollen. Her usually chubby cheeks puffed to twice their normal size. There were adhesive marks where masks and tubes had been taped down and where doctors had propped her mouth open. Everything she must have been feeling was scary or strange. When Lizzie's eyes flickered open for a moment, there was no recognition there. "She's still pretty out of it," the nurse reminded us. "Just give her time."

For the next five days, Ken and I stayed by Lizzie's side. This was a busy city hospital. On the pediatric floor, there were no private rooms for cases like ours. We were issued a crib, a table, and a single chair. Ken filched another chair from a room down the hall. But for nearly a week, at least one of us was with Lizzie for every moment. Looking back, I don't recall how we passed the time. Like the people in the waiting room, we packed books we did not read and brought work we did not do. The hospital screened movies we did not watch and offered parenting groups we did not attend. One afternoon, I remember a chaplain making the rounds and asking if I wanted to pray. I nodded my head but did not speak. I was seated in our chair holding a sleeping Lizzie gently on my lap. The nurses preferred that Lizzie sleep in her crib, as she was attached to an oxygen mask and an IV. But in the crib, she cried, even in her sleep, and the whimpering quieted more easily into rest when I held her. So I did that almost constantly. The chaplain put his hand on my shoulder and mumbled in hushed tones. I thanked him with another nod, and he left.

Lizzie did not drink any milk while in the hospital. After so many months of trying to feed her, it was disconcerting to pump milk she could, once again, not ingest. The nurses on the ward helped find us a freezer to store it to bring home. Lizzie was given fluids through an IV. A pulse oximeter attached to her finger monitored her heartbeat and the oxygen levels in her bloodstream. Nurses taught me how to adminis- ter pain medications with a soft eye dropper along the inside of Lizzie's cheek, keeping her head tilted backward and her mouth closed so she would swallow, no matter how uncomfortable she was. It reminded me of how we had given medicine to our family cat, Pepper, when I was a kid. But unlike Pepper, Lizzie never clawed or bit. She just laid in my lap and occasionally drooled pink medicine onto her chin. I learned to chart medications myself and communicate with the nurses half an hour before Lizzie was due for them so the pain did not creep up on us. I learned to sleep hunched forward in the chair with my head on the edge of Lizzie's mattress so that she always knew I was there.

And then, just like that, we were informed we were being released. After our previous premature exit from a hospital, with a child too dangerously lethargic to nurse, I was horrified to hear that we were being sent home with the *expectation* that Lizzie would sleep constantly and not eat. Unlike that first time around, I was now hypervigilant about what-ifs and best- and worst-case scenarios. I wanted to know what to look for and when to be concerned. I wanted daytime phone numbers and nighttime phone numbers and a follow-up with her surgeons in DC before we journeyed back to Ohio. And no one thought I was crazy. Everyone understood. Doctors explained that Lizzie's appetite would return slowly. She would be able to swallow normally within a week or two. And unlike when she was a newborn, they assured me that because we had fed her so well and grown her so strong, her body could handle this brief disruption in nourishment. *She would be okay.*

We left the hospital with a sheaf of discharge instruction papers and advice on which baby paraphernalia to buy to monitor Lizzie's breathing while she slept. And we left with hope. That night, we stayed in a friend's basement guest room, and Lizzie even sat up to play with toys on the carpet. We followed up with the doctors the following morning, and by noon, we were on the road home.

Lizzie slept for the entire six-hour drive back to Cleveland. I woke her once to get a medicine dropper full of Tylenol into her, and then she drifted back to sleep. Once again, we were driving away from a hospital with a baby who could not eat. But the parallels ended there. Unlike our floppy and sleepy days-old infant, six-month-old Lizzie was a fighter. The drugs made her loopy, and her mouth surely ached, but this time, she would let us know how she felt. Perhaps because of the change in her airway or maybe because of her immediate need to communicate, Lizzie began to make the sound I will always consider her first word. She shrieked it when she first woke up. She wailed it when she was hungry or scared or mad or sleepy. It was a single announcement repeated over and over. The configuration of most babies' mouths and airways makes *da-da, da-da* the most natural first babble. But for Lizzie, her first utterance was "mahmi-ya, mahmi-ya, mahmi-ya." She did not learn any new words for many, many months to come. And I'm not sure she even understood those sounds as words until much later. But I heard her. And I knew she was asking for me.

Recovery 2

After a few days at home, Lizzie began to take milk again. She was voracious, a little girl making up for lost time. And food. As the doctors predicted, her mouth began to heal. Ken returned to work, which had him gone all the time. So I did my best to be both a mother and a father to our two children.

Though I have been a bookworm all my life, I did not read a single volume for the first year of Lizzie's life. Though I have always enjoyed exercise, I did not lift weights, attend yoga classes, or even walk my dogs. And though I had been a teacher, a writer, a counselor, a fundraiser, and a friend, I buried those talents and cared solely for my girls.

Single-handedly meeting the needs of those two kids often felt like more work than caring for 125 high school students. Winter in Ohio proved a difficult time to make friends. Katie and I played a lot of Barbies, and Lizzie disrupted many games of Candy Land. We slogged through snow to check out library books and wandered down to the river to feed stale sandwich bread to the ducks and swans. Katie played fashion show with her closet full of dresses and Mommy-horse on my post-pregnancy back. We played Restaurant, a game which involved allowing Katie to concoct alarming food combinations—graham cracker sandwiches with basil leaves and butter, pickle juice smoothies, lettuce soup—while Lizzie and I pretended to be her customers. I helped Katie design a leprechaun catcher and a bird feeder, and I tackled the myriad other responsibilities that come with solo-parenting a preschooler. I was determined to care for Katie in ways I had not been able to in Virginia while still tending to Lizzie. I modeled the pre-speech ululations her doctor recommended, pureed her soft vegetables and bananas, and still awoke to feed her every night between two and three o'clock.

My mom friends sometimes complain about having trouble sleeping. I guess they lie awake and worry about their kids, home repair, and money. Perhaps I had similar concerns, but parenting alone during the week, I was too tired even to dream about them. I fell asleep moments after my head hit the pillow.

And then, just like that, Lizzie was a year old. Her scars healed. Her feeding difficulties ended.

 **8**   EVERY STORM ENDS

And then, just like that, Lizzie was a year old. Her scars healed. Her feeding difficulties ended. And though she would require several more surgeries in upcoming years, for the time being, she was a perfectly happy child. She was active and curious. She held onto furniture and scooted up and down stairs. Whenever I cooked, she opened the bottom kitchen drawer and took out all the Tupperware or pulled out tissues, one by one, until they were heaped in a feathery white pile beside an empty Kleenex box. And while her vocal patterns were unorthodox—very nasal and full of strange sound compensations, like a throaty *k* instead of *s*—we had a speech therapist come to our home every week who worked with Lizzie to get breath and sounds coming out of her mouth instead of her nose. I had been skeptical of intervention for a child so young, but Ms. Ashley used bubbles and pinwheels, interactive games, toys, and books to coax Lizzie to say *puh* and *duh* and *dah-dah* and the handful of other sounds that were second nature to other toddlers but which our child needed to be taught.

With Lizzie on the mend and Katie transitioning into kindergarten, I felt that familiar itch to balance the imbalance and venture back to work outside of my home. I longed for the company of other adults. And I felt the need to demonstrate to my girls that a woman could wear more than one hat.

At first, I envisioned going back to teaching. But with Lizzie's countless medical appointments and Katie's limited school hours, even a part-time gig would require additional childcare and constant juggling. I needed more flexibility and fewer hours. Just something to offset the constant family grind. Which is how I found Maggie's Place.

Following Lizzie's first surgery, our church, St. Joan of Arc—where we were brand new parishioners—began delivering meals to us. Families I had never laid eyes upon came to the door with roasted chickens, mashed potatoes, and arugula salads. Moms brought coloring books and quilts and asked whether they could mind the baby while I napped or grabbed a shower. These strangers swaddled us in kindness and help before we even asked. I was embarrassed at first, but the relief kept coming, so eventually, I learned to accept it with a grateful heart. Just after Lizzie's first birthday when a mom friend from church asked for volunteers to bring meals and supplies to other mothers in need, I signed up. I wanted to teach my girls the importance of paying it forward.

Once a month, we loaded our minivans with clothes, baby supplies, toiletries, and homemade salads and casseroles and drove out of our little bubble of a village to spend the evening at a center for pregnant women. The idea was that moms like us—women with children and bounty and a roof over our heads—would ease the burden of moms like them—young girls living in a transitional home for pregnancy support and post-partum care.

Some of these women were battling addiction. Others were running from abuse. Still others simply had nowhere else to go. We sought to bring these moms-to-be a bit of ease, sharing stories, recounting blessings, and breaking bread. Because Ken was away, I usually made a point of bringing my children along. I thought Katie might enjoy playing waitress among these strangers and sharing the food we had cooked together. I knew it would be good for her to set someone else's table for a change. Lizzie could toddle into the playroom or sit in my lap and charm the other moms with her smiles.

Perhaps my children sensed my desire to show them off, because they seemed to go out of their way to misbehave and embarrass me every chance they got. Katie knocked a drink onto a newborn's face, ate the brownies we had reserved for the pregnant mothers, and asked one postpartum mommy if the baby had *come out where she peed.* Though usually an even-tempered child, Lizzie cried and fussed and spit up and often hid under the table while the adults said grace. As my girls got older, they staged games of freeze tag in the sleeping quarters and were forever making messes in the community room that they did not wish to clean up.

I could trace some of these behaviors back to our home. In the hours before heading to Maggie's Place, Katie and I, along with little Lizzie, experienced something that could only be called kitchen apocalypse. We were often preparing meals for fifteen to twenty people. Despite several years of college calculus, I never could successfully quadruple a recipe. And despite acing high school geometry, I repeatedly underestimated how much batter or stew or sauce could fit in any one bowl, pot, or pan. Sprinkle that with a lifelong difficulty with judging how long any single task is likely to take and toss a few hungry children into that mix, and it was not unusual to see every single inch of counter space covered with something dirty, crying, or broken—or for me to forget to feed my children before we sprinted out the door. They often arrived at Maggie's Place exhausted and hungry, and then I was surprised when they did not perform well on command.

In the beginning, I went to Maggie's Place because I thought I would bring comfort to the women there. After all, while our circumstances were not the same, my family had just been through quite an ordeal with Lizzie. We had moved twice in less than a year, we had struggled to care for our baby, and I was often parenting my children alone. Perhaps my story did bring these women a bit of comfort. (Though, more likely, that came in the form of soup or chicken or bread.) Many of these young ladies had every reason to feel downtrodden. They had no jobs, no home, a harried past, and an uncertain future. Their love for their babies had ruined some of their plans. But I also saw how that love liberated them. Those babies unearthed in their mamas a quiet determination and a fierce protective spirit. Jackie*, one young woman I got to know, had been a middling student until the birth of her son. But now that she was a mother, she no longer allowed herself the luxury of poor school performance. She completed her GED while her son napped. She enrolled in community college night classes and applied to work at a local sandwich shop during the day. She reconciled her relationship with her own mother. And Jackie did all of that to give her child opportunities that she had not had. Her story, and the stories of so many women like her, inspired me to view my time at home with my children in a better light.

In the faces of these strangers, I discovered kinship and acceptance.

Over the years, I continued to journey to Maggie's Place, because these women brought comfort to me. They taught me to cherish my kids more. What a blessing it was to be with them. And how fleeting those days of mothering young children really were. I even grew to appreciate my kids' poor behavior.

5 Talk to Strangers

It humbled me. I was not there to show off my perfect life to these moms. I was not there to teach them all the answers. I had my own imbalances to contend with. In the faces of these strangers, I discovered kinship and acceptance. It would have been easy to stay in our village and keep to our well-traveled paths. But talking to strangers was better. These mothers helped me realize that while I had given up a lot to stay with my girls, being at home also freed me. Being with my kids and journeying to Maggie's Place helped me think more deeply about what it meant to be a teacher, a writer, a counselor, a fundraiser, and a friend. I realized that—whether I was in the classroom full time or not—I was still able to share those gifts with others and demonstrate them to my children. Becoming a mother did not mean I buried my talents; becoming a mother helped me unearth them.

*Name has been changed.

8: Wintering in Saskatchewan

The move to Chagrin Falls felt too perfect to be real. At long last, we had found our safe harbor. Our kitchen window overlooked the river, and whenever it rained, we could hear the upper set of waterfalls crashing just out of sight. The heart of town was a three-minute stroll away, past painstakingly restored Victorian homes and neighbors who waved without fail. The family-run hardware store also sold fishing bait, the café served breakfast anytime, and on weekends, visitors toured the village in a horse-drawn carriage. There was a library and a playground nestled right next to the falls. And upstream, the lazy, rock-bottomed Chagrin River became an endless source of adventure for the girls. Katie and Lizzie learned how to catch crawfish there, first with a net, then, when they were a little braver, with their bare hands. They made teeter-totters out of fallen trees and swam in the bubbling currents. And when they weren't adventuring, they socialized. They played on soccer teams, sang in the children's choir at church, and made friends. After our tiny Virginia cottage, our three-story Ohio house seemed like a mansion. There were two staircases for playing chase and a bay window big enough to use as a talent show stage. The girls had their own rooms, with a Jack-and-Jill closet that ran in between. They called it their secret passageway. Katie pretended it led to Narnia.

Our new home had it all. Almost. The only thing missing was me. Most weeks, my consulting job kept me on the road from Monday morning through Thursday night, helping some faraway Fortune 500 company grow its bottom line. I wore button-down shirts and used words like "leverage" and "synergy." And though I worked hard to serve my clients, it was a far cry from tracking war criminals in Afghanistan or helping fellow veterans regain a sense of purpose. This was not my dream job. But at that point, what our family needed was financial stability and health care. We needed a way to pay our mounting medical bills and make sure Lizzie had the best doctors in the world. And on that, the firm delivered.

Almost overnight, the stress of those medical expenses was gone. We had scheduled Lizzie's first surgery months in advance with no real understanding of how much it would cost. Now, with me working this consulting job, we could pay for it. And Annmarie and the girls were content. I tried to convince myself that this new normal could last. I might not have been saving the world, but I did have a purpose. I was providing financially for my family. If that meant four, sometimes five or six, days a week on the road, so be it. Lots of dads had it worse. Some much worse, like the friends I left in the military who were gone for months on end, risking their lives and earning a fraction of what I made.

I did not form close ties with many consulting colleagues. Aside from the job, we did not have much in common. I was older than most associates. I did not have a business degree, and I was not using the consulting firm as a stepping stone for a career in management. There were a few older partners that I did befriend. They had kids, and we talked from time to time about how they balanced family life against the grueling work schedule. All too often, the answer boiled down to money. Bigger houses, country club memberships, the best summer camps for the kids. Almost everyone had a gardener. It made sense. If a parent could not be around, at least they could prove the time away was worth something, like an inground pool.

Too often, however, the things my colleagues used to justify their work schedules became traps. Fancy cars need fancy car payments. McMansions beget McMortgages. I saw it happen all the time: friends climbing the rungs at the firm or in the businesses we served who considered the idea of starting a nonprofit or going into teaching or doing something they really loved. But their lives put up walls, built brick by brick from the *things* they could not do without, like the new Audi, the kitchen remodel, the yearly trip to Bermuda. So they stuck with it, stayed on the treadmill, and never discovered real purpose beyond providing things for those they loved. The saddest symptom of this was the presents. Not the Christmas or birthday gifts (which were sometimes over the top) but the stuffed animals and video games hastily purchased from airport kiosks to make up for missing a ball game or school musical. A few parents I knew bought something for their kids every time they traveled. I now understand the real reason airports have toy stores in them. And it breaks my heart.

Seeing all this, I was determined to keep those same walls from closing in. I kept my old car. We did not hire a gardener. And I did not bring home presents from every trip as if they could compensate for me being gone. Though I struggled to explain to Katie why this job was important for our family, I tried to share some of what I was doing. Everywhere I went, I kept hotel key cards. I gave them to my kids, and I told them about my travels. They were curious about my work world, even the mundane details. They always asked if my hotel had a swimming pool. Usually, the answer was yes. And whether I had swum in it. The answer was always no. They wondered about the towns I visited. Was Columbus, Ohio, fun? What was Peoria, Illinois, like in winter? Answer—flat, cold, and white. I did my best to share with them, but there was not always very much to say about the world I left them for.

A year into the gig, I was asked to go to Saskatchewan, Canada, to help a mining company pull more stuff out of the ground. On paper, it looked like the worst job ever. Nobody at the firm wanted it. I, on the other hand, was so tired of crunching numbers that I decided to take a chance—with one condition: I wanted to get my hands dirty. I convinced my managers that to understand the client's operations, I needed to learn the mining business close up. Truth is, I wanted to escape my desk.

Even though the job took me farther from Annmarie and the kids than any other assignment with the firm, my time in Saskatchewan turned out to be the best thing I did in my two years as a consultant. That is, if you ignore the most epic commute in Harbaugh family history. I left home every Sunday for the two-leg red-eye to Regina, Saskatchewan. Then I rented a car for a nearly four-hour drive to reach the mine by sunrise. The highway was so desolate that I packed a survival kit in case I ran off the road or got stuck in a snowdrift—or hit a moose, which happened to more than a few of my mining buddies. The reverse commute on Friday delivered me home in time for an abbreviated weekend with the family. Come Sunday night, I repeated the whole thing.

Mining was my kind of gig, though. I was surrounded by people I understood. We swore, drank, and did the kind of work that got dirt under our nails. We laughed off the Saskatchewan cold and looked forward to those warm hours underground. More than once, I had to pee on my car door handle to thaw it enough to open it. I was invited on snowmobile trips to distant ice-fishing holes (which I accepted) and to dwarf-throwing contests at the only bar in town (which I declined). I got to do things most high-paid business consultants never get to do, like weld steel brackets while suspended halfway down a mile-deep mineshaft. I knew I was finally accepted into the brotherhood of miners when they left me alone in the darkness at the end of a mile-long underground tunnel with nothing for company but my own nightmares of being crushed alive. That was my initiation. I felt valued, helping make dangerous work safer for people I cared about.

One of my bosses talked about my ability to translate. It wasn't that I spoke flawless Canadian. Rather, I had a knack for helping the above-ground business types understand the problems below. When the miners complained that three thousand unsafe brackets needed to be redesigned,

I threw on some clean pants and a button-down shirt, walked into corporate HQ, and explained how giving the workers what they needed would make the company more profitable in the long run.

During the brief weekends at home, I did my best to fight off fatigue and make the most of my moments with the kids. Once the snow thawed in Ohio, we embarked on day-long upriver expeditions with a dry bag full of extra clothes, a mini camp stove, a water filter, and a box of mac'n'cheese. We made our camp at the river's edge, put the macaroni on to boil, and set out to catch a pot of crawfish. We cooked them up in the hot noodle water until they turned bright red and delicious.

The girls and I sure had our moments. Some great ones. Like the time they caught the snake and made Daddy hold it even though snakes are the ONLY CREATURES IN THE WORLD he thinks are completely unnecessary. Still, my memory of those times is intermittent, like a slideshow (or, rather, a PowerPoint presentation, which I was getting pretty good at). Unlike Annmarie, I was only getting snapshots, missing the full video of the girls growing up. In between those frames were long stretches of important moments where I was totally out of the picture. Like Katie's first soccer game, or Lizzie's first day of preschool, or the father-daughter spaghetti dinner where the kids' artwork was on display for every proud dad to see. Except one.

Part of me resented Annmarie for all the time she had with the kids. My rational side understood that being a mother of two was not easy. I nevertheless envied the life she and the girls were living without me. One symptom of that separation was the nickname I gave Elizabeth. For the two years I worked as a consultant, I called her "Ellie." Everyone else—Annmarie, Katie, grandparents, teachers, friends—knew her as their little "Lizzie." I held fast to the nickname I gave her in the hospital the first time I held her in my arms as the nurse pointed out the hole in the back of her throat. She was my Ellie, no matter what anyone said. It was my obstinate way of not surrendering every aspect of parenting to Annmarie.

Winter in Saskatchewan is bleak and cold, but I made the most of it. When not underground, I explored the frozen wilderness on skis under a giant kite pulled along by the wind. Snowkiting was my escape, my chance to be free of everything but the wind and snow. On clear evenings, the moon lit the ground silver. Sometimes, on the blackest of nights, the Northern Lights put on a show and the aurora illuminated my path home. As much as I missed Annmarie and the girls, I found enough excitement and purpose in Saskatchewan to keep me going. And when the darkness grew too long and I grew too lonely, I wrote stories for my daughters. I invented a character named Katie McElliegot, a little girl who sailed a boat around the world, searching for her dad. Every few weeks, I finished a chapter and emailed it to Annmarie. She stayed up late to read aloud as Katie and Ellie fell asleep, dreaming of their namesake heroine sailing through storms and past sea serpents on the adventure of a lifetime.

Double Bottom Line

Eventually, the mining job came to an end. Even winter in Saskatchewan could not last forever. I knew no other consulting gig could match what I found working a mile underground in the middle of the Canadian wilderness. Sure enough, the firm assigned me to a pharmaceutical company next. The commute was fifteen hours shorter, but the work was, to say the least, unfulfilling. I began to ask, "Is what I did today worth not tucking my kids in tonight?" The answer was, usually, "No."

I had committed to the firm a full two years of my life and was determined to follow through. They had been good to me: they had taken care of my family, Lizzie's surgeries, and her endless consults and therapy sessions. The paychecks felt good, too. But I knew that if I was going to be away, I needed to find a job that was worth falling asleep alone. So, two years to the day after I signed up, I left. When I shared the news with Katie, she smiled, hugged me, and ran to her room. Moments later, she returned with her collection of hotel key cards. I don't know how many were in the stack, but it had to be close to a hundred. "Can I get rid of these now?" she asked.

I took a job with a veterans' advocacy group based in Washington, DC. The travel was almost as bad, but the work felt better. It was by no means a perfect job, but it was a step closer. One of the things I was proudest of was launching a campaign to change the way Americans perceive veterans. We called it Got Your 6, which was military-speak for "I've got your back." The idea was simple—convince Hollywood to change the way it tells stories about vets. Use actual veterans, real-life portrayals, to convince Americans that the veteran next door is an asset to their community, not a liability.

We enlisted the help of some pretty big names: Tom Hanks, Taylor Swift, Harrison Ford. We even got Michelle Obama and the penguins from *Madagascar* to do an educational video about veterans coming back to their communities. More importantly, we convinced the most innovative veterans' nonprofits to come on board to shape the story we wanted to tell. The Mission Continues was one of those organizations. So was a much smaller outfit named Team Rubicon. Their mission was to take motivated military veterans with skills and experiences sharpened in Iraq and Afghanistan and turn them into disaster relief workers. The group had started in Haiti in the aftermath of the massive 2010 earthquake when two Marine sergeants saw the devastation on TV and realized that it looked eerily similar to what they had seen in Iraq and Afghanistan. Jake Wood and Will McNulty were determined to help. They pulled together an eight-man team of combat medics and surgeons and within forty-eight hours were in Port-au-Prince saving lives. The skills they brought to bear, as disciplined and organized military veterans, made them stand out amidst the chaos of the relief effort. Within seventy-two hours of their arrival, their small team was tasked with running the largest hospital in the Haitian capital.

By the time I started paying attention to Team Rubicon, they had a few hundred members. Got Your 6 gave them some publicity and a little funding and even sent them a young intern named Sean to help with the minutiae of launching a nonprofit. In his first week, he sent back a simple but compelling report.

"These guys are going to change the world," Sean said. "Also, they sure do use the F word a lot." I guess saving lives gets you a pass on that kind of thing.

I loved working with veterans, but, once again, the job kept me away from the girls. "These are formative years," Annmarie said. "Don't miss them." So especially with Katie, I made sure to keep the kids involved in what I was doing. As the leader of a DC-based advocacy group, I received an invitation to President Obama's second inauguration. I wrangled one extra ticket and brought Katie with me. She sat on my shoulders as President Obama took the oath of office. The crowd stretched as far as the eye could see, an ocean of tiny American flags, each held by a fellow citizen bearing witness to democracy in action. There were over a million people on the National Mall that day. Politics aside, it was an inspiring moment for father and daughter alike. We listened to Beyoncé sing the national anthem and talked about how so many different Americans, from so many different parts of the country, could come together to honor an idea.

The job certainly came with purpose and even the occasional adventure. Because of the Hollywood stuff, I often traveled to Los Angeles and once had to cross the entire country for a single two-hour meeting.

"This is ridiculous," I complained to Annmarie as I packed for the trip. "Ten hours on a plane for *one meeting!*"

"Make the most of it, then," she said.

Then she threw out an idea that was, quite possibly, even more ridiculous than crossing a continent to meet with a movie star.

So I packed another bag, bought an extra ticket with airline points, and extended the trip for two days. On my way to the airport, I stopped by Katie's school. With a secondhand wetsuit slung over my shoulder, I signed in at the front desk and told them what I was doing. Then I walked right into her second grade classroom.

"Hey, Katie, wanna go to California?" I said.

She was blown away.

I went to my meeting in Los Angeles while a friend took Katie to the Santa Monica pier. The rest of the time, Katie and I had LA all to ourselves. We ate seafood in Newport, watched the crazy bodybuilders at Muscle Beach, and kept an eye out for famous people. Best of all, we surfed. Every morning as the sun came up over the city, we headed down to the beach with our rented boards and paddled out. The waves could not have been more perfect—waist high with gently peeling lips that broke in knee-deep water; I could give Katie a lesson while standing up. Within five minutes, she was catching her own waves and riding them all the way to the sand.

We carried our boards back to the hotel room, both exhausted and refreshed.

"Think we could live here?" I asked her.

"Yeah," she said. "I wish we could do this all the time."

As much as I loved the new job working for vets, and as hard as I tried to inject a sense of adventure for me and the kids, Katie knew what was missing. Nothing could take the place of being together.

FEELING LUCKY

There are some experiences in my life that I choose to bury: a few from Afghanistan that I keep hidden away; the closed-casket funeral in high school for the friend who shot himself. Deepest of all is the memory of Lizzie's second surgery, the moment I let her down when she needed me most.

Now that she was two and a half, she was strong enough for a much longer operation involving four separate procedures. In our preoperative briefs, the surgeons were matter-of-fact, even casual. We asked each to explain in detail what would happen and what might go wrong. One of them described how the fatty-tissue graft might be rejected and that there was nothing to do except wait and see. He added, "That's pretty rare, though. And if it does happen, I'll probably publish a paper about it, if that's all right with you." I wore my consultant's hat to each of these meetings. I asked tough questions and did not mind tough answers. Annmarie and I decided early on that we did not need doctors who were gentle and kind. We needed experts with scalpels. If they were arrogant, we did not care, as long as they were good at what they did.

Lizzie's first surgery, when she was just six months old, was supposed to be the bad one. Her mouth was so tiny, her body so wiry. One doctor advised us against it, explaining that Lizzie's procedure, a *z-furlough closure*, should happen much later, when her body was bigger and stronger and there was more room in her throat for the surgeon to operate. But we had one of the best teams in the world working on Lizzie's case, including a doctor who had pioneered the procedure in infants. The sooner her palate was repaired, he explained, the sooner she could learn to talk normally. Lizzie's recovery was by no means easy, but even as a six-month-old, her toughness surprised everyone.

Annmarie carried her to the operating table that time. She sang to Lizzie and ran a hand over her forehead while the anesthesia took her under. My wife seemed so strong, so confident shepherding our baby through those swinging double doors into the OR. When she walked back into the waiting room, after the nurses had taken over, she broke down in my arms. The other parents looked up then went back to whatever they were doing. They understood.

As we geared up for the second surgery, Annmarie was emphatic. "I cannot do that again," she said. She was pregnant again and claimed she felt too emotional to be strong for Lizzie.

"You don't have to," I said. I promised to hold Lizzie's hand, to be brave as long as I needed to be.

"It's going to be harder than you think," Annmarie warned me. "The room itself—the beeping, the floodlights, the strangers in masks—you have to steel yourself for it."

I thought I could do it. I *knew* I could do it. I was not the faint-hearted type. Hadn't I brought that just-the-facts attitude to every surgical consult? From no-nonsense Navy pilot to dispassionate business consultant, if there was one emotion I had mastered, it was being *non*emotional.

Annmarie, Lizzie, and I arrived at the hospital while it was still dark outside. Her surgery was the first of the day. With multiple doctors scrubbing in, and with the difficulty of predicting the length of each procedure, the early morning time slot seemed the best way to minimize complications. Lizzie and I changed into surgical gowns, and I made a joke about butts. She smiled, wanly. Unlike the first time around, Lizzie was now two years old. She understood things. She had questions. Though she was accustomed to hospitals and waiting rooms, she knew something was different that morning. We told her the doctors were going to take care of her ears, teeth, and mouth so that she did not get sick. But she remained unconvinced. We sat with our books, listening for the charge nurse to tell us it was time. Despite Annmarie's pep talk, I felt an oncoming dread. As much as I wanted to get this over with, I was also terrified of hearing the nurse call Lizzie's name.

Annmarie sensed it. "Be brave," she whispered. "Take some deep breaths." The sooner we walked through those double doors, the sooner we would be done.

Lizzie's name flashed on a monitor above the waiting room desk. Moments later, a nurse entered. She glanced at her clipboard and said, "Elizabeth Harbaugh?" Annmarie gave my hand a squeeze. I lifted Lizzie off my lap and held her hand as we followed the nurse into the brightly lit hallway that led to the operating theater. Someone told me to put on my mask. Entering the OR, everything was as Annmarie had warned: the strangers, the lights, the machines. I lifted Lizzie onto the operating table. She held my neck and buried her face in my shoulder. She was too frightened to cry or even whimper. Annmarie's words rang in my ears: *Be brave.*

I paused, still bent over the operating table with Lizzie clutching me tightly.

"Sir," one of the nurses said, "we need to put this on her face."

Out of the corner of my eye, I saw a clear plastic mask with a hose attached. I pried Lizzie's face from my shoulder, enough for the nurse to slip the mask between. Lizzie loosened her grip on me and reached to pull off the mask.

"Sir, that cannot come off," a nurse said. "We'll have to restrain her if she keeps pulling on it."

I held Lizzie's arms down and kept my forehead pressed to hers. "It's okay, sweetheart," I said. Her eyes were wide open, bigger than I'd ever seen them. She was staring into mine an inch away, and I could see the panic taking over. I began to sing. Her favorite lullaby, the one I used to get her to fall asleep.

"Go to sleep, my little Ellie . . ."

She clutched me tighter, her eyes pleading.

"Go to sleep, my little Ellie . . ."

It was not just fear I saw but betrayal.

"You and me and your mama make three . . ."

I could not finish. I saw her eyes flutter, but not soon enough. The next lines of the song stuck in my throat. I began to cry. In that final moment, what she needed was my strength and reassurance. Instead, the last thing she saw in my eyes was fear. As her arms went limp and her eyes rolled back, I could only think of how I had failed her.

I was still crying when I walked into the waiting room, but I did not talk about how I had left Lizzie. In fact, the first time I confessed it to Annmarie was during the writing of this book. As a father, I felt as though it was my job to never demonstrate weakness or fear. I had this idea that dads are the strong ones. Which I have realized is ridiculous. And unfair. When it comes to keeping a brave face in front of our kids, my wife is the rock. I am now okay admitting that.

Many hours later, we met Lizzie in the recovery room. Her face was swollen, and there was dried blood around her lips. We spent the next three days in the hospital, longer than we had planned. The surgery had gone well, but Lizzie was stubborn and in pain, and she would not play by the nurses' rules. She refused to take her medicine, refused to drink fluids, and ripped off her pulse oximeter repeatedly. Five hours under the knife, and our little girl came back fighting mad. As frustrated as we may have been with her failure to cooperate, Annmarie and I could not help but be awed by Lizzie's strength.

There was a vinyl couch in her hospital room, so Annmarie and I took turns sleeping by Lizzie's side. We did our best to get medicine into her. She needed those painkillers to numb her enough to be able to swallow. We tried to explain that if she could not drink, she could not go home. The IV could not stay taped to her arm forever.

We may have borne the burdens of caring for her differently—I worked long hours in a mine to ensure we had health care while Annmarie tended to the home front—but we were a team.

As Annmarie and I took turns holding Lizzie in our arms, comforting her, singing

 4 Imbalance is Balance

her to sleep, I felt myself letting go of something I had been clinging to since the day she was born. My nickname for her, Ellie, the one I alone had used, seemed unnecessary now. I had held onto it as a way of preserving a special bond with my little girl. But as the hours dragged on in that recovery room, it became clear that there was nothing competitive in Annmarie's and my love for this child. We may have borne the burdens of caring for her differently—I worked long hours in a mine to ensure we had health care while Annmarie tended to the home front—but we were a team.

When I sang my song again, the one I tried to finish in the OR, it finally sounded right.

Go to sleep, my little Lizzie . . . Go to sleep, my little Lizzie . . .

On the morning of the second day, Annmarie asked me to go to the Ronald McDonald House across the street. She pointed out that it made no sense for both of us to be in Lizzie's room while she rested, especially since there was only the one couch for us to sleep on.

I made my way through the labyrinthine hospital and over to the Ronald McDonald House. At the reception desk, a kind old man welcomed me.

"Fridge is stocked," he said. "Grab whatever you want. Eat in the dining room, please. Your room is just down the hall." He handed me a form to sign and a set of keys.

Annmarie and I were exhausted, but at the end of this ordeal, we would bring our little girl home.

 **8** Every Storm Ends

My accommodations were plain, the furnishings donated. It was nothing like the fancy hotel rooms I had grown accustomed to as a consultant. Against the wall was a simple writing desk with a guest book on it. I flipped it open, sat on the bed, and began reading. Page after page was filled with notes from parents who stayed before me. Most of them recorded simple thank-you notes for the chance to spend a night in a real bed and eat a home-cooked meal delivered by an invisible army of volunteers. Some of the entries were longer, though—from parents emptying their hearts.

One started with the line *Our little boy, Ethan, died today.*

I left the Ronald McDonald House early the next morning, thankful for the night's rest but even more grateful for the perspective my stay had given me. On the way out, I exchanged glances with another father. There was a connection, however fleeting, as if we both knew something about love that few other parents could fathom. We smiled and nodded but avoided small talk, fearful that even the simplest conversation could rupture into heartbreak.

For the first time in a long while, I felt lucky. Lizzie was in pain, but she would get better. Annmarie and I were exhausted, but at the end of this ordeal, we would bring our little girl home. Whatever my failings as a father, I was indeed blessed, and my beautiful family was intact.

And we were about to add one more.

9: Biggest

Not long ago, Lizzie handed me a sketch of a large, round person surrounded by at least a dozen scraggly kittens. "Who's this?" I asked.

"That's you," she said. "When Henry was in your belly."

"Really?" I replied. "And where did all these cats come from?"

"Your butt!" she said and ran away giggling before I could swat her on her own behind.

Lizzie's understanding of mammalian reproductive parts may have been shoddy, but the rest of her recollection was spot on. I am a hefty pregnant woman. Some women carry entirely in their bellies. They wear flouncy sundresses and wry *Got Milk?* t-shirts over their baby bumps. From the rear, they can still be mistaken for Pilates instructors or ballroom dancers. Not me. My last pregnancy was visible from all angles. Sure, my belly looked pregnant, but so did my knees. And my ankles. And my nose.

Lizzie actually coined a new word—*hunormous*—to describe my super-sized physique. When I visited Katie's classroom for the Mother's Day tea, her teacher insisted I sit in her own personal chair. When I took the girls to an indoor playground, I got stuck between two foam rollers at the entrance. On the drive to my baby shower, a friend had to buckle my sandals. I was a big girl.

Which is why it was all the more impressive that, other than one brief altercation with someone's grandmother over the parking space she stole from me in front of the ice cream stand, I was not particularly temperamental or unreasonable. Despite looking like a medium-sized toolshed, I largely kept my cool.

Until the last little bit.

Past Due

When I passed my due date, I felt the crazy coming on. Statistically speaking, a woman is far more likely to give birth a day or two before her due date, or a few days after, rather than precisely on it. The math makes sense. But toward the end of that pregnancy, math was not my strong suit. I fixated on that due date. It became my beacon, my mantra, that red triangle guiding me into safe harbor.

> *On April 24th, I can sleep on my tummy again.*
> *On April 24th, the heartburn will stop.*
> *On April 24th, I will be able to buckle my shoes.*

If pregnancy is like a marathon, the due date is the finish line. And when you get to the due date without a baby, it is as though you have run that race only to discover that it's been extended. Instead of twenty-six miles, you'll be running twenty-eight. Instead of nine months pregnant, I was working on ten.

And so I developed a few *sensitivities* toward the end of my pregnancy. After so long feeling large and unwieldy, after so many weeks of being the elephant in the room . . . well, I got to the point where there were a few things I preferred folks not say to me:

1. "You look like you are ready to pop." Ah, yes. The clever balloon metaphor. This was the preferred comment of the furnace

inspector, both mattress deliverymen, and several husbands of women I hardly knew. For some reason, it seemed appropriate to all of those people to tell me I looked so large that I might explode. I felt like replying: "You look like you are ready to be kicked in the face." Ken tried to appease me: "I don't think they meant *pop* so much as *pop out*, you know, like the little red thermometer on the Thanksgiving turkey." With that explanation, my own husband took his place in the face-kicking line. Pregnant or not, no woman wishes to be compared to poultry.

2. "I didn't even notice you were pregnant." When people said this to me, I think they were trying to be kind. You know, *Nobody mention the blimp-sized woman in the corner.* And yes, in a fair universe, if I did not wish to be told how large I looked, this ought to have been a safe remark. But once I passed that due date, I had gained SIXTY-FIVE pounds—a disproportionate amount of it in my chin. It horrified me to think that anyone would suggest that I looked the same as I always had.

3. "Do you have any names in mind?" I know, I know. What could be wrong with such a benign inquiry? This is such a classic conversation starter. We have all used it. But here's the thing: once a woman has been pregnant for what can easily be rounded up to a year, she has answered this question almost daily for the duration. She has been queried about the name of her child hundreds of times. Once I passed my due date, I started making things up. "I just *love* the name Balthazar, don't you?" Or "Xerxes is my husband's name, so we are thinking of naming this one Xerxes Jr." I got so tired of answering the name question that I started thinking of whatever names sounded the worst with Ken's last name—Herbert, Harper, Arlo. "It will either be Marvin or Hobart," I would say. "Hobart Harbaugh . . ." my well-meaning inquisitor would repeat, stumbling a little on the *H*s and *B*s. "That's . . . lovely." Because another dumb thing about the name

line of questioning is that there is nothing you can say in reply except, "That's an awesome name." Even if the name is terrible. Even if it reminds you of your ex-boyfriend, Herbert, who cheated on you with one of the lunch ladies at school, you can't say that. Even if the name "Arlo Harbaugh" sounds like a person who would flunk the second grade or be mauled by a bear, you can't say that. When couples tell you what they are naming their child, you have a near-constitutional obligation to say: "Nice name." Even if it's not. I figured if people were going to have to lie after they heard the name we had chosen, it was only fair that I could lie, too. Of course, looking back, it seems a little mean to have fibbed about the name of my precious, unborn child. I can only ask forgiveness. Maybe when a person's body is swollen and misshapen, the brain follows suit.

4. "Are you having a boy or a girl?" Of all things people said to me throughout my pregnancy, this one took the cake. Again, it was a seemingly innocuous question, but the roads it led us down were dicey . . .

Ken, the kids, and I were eating at a Red Robin one afternoon, and a woman walked by our table on her way to the bathroom. "Congratulations," she said, pointing to me. At first, I thought she was applauding my selection of the Angus patty with bacon and arugula, but then she continued. "Do you know what you are having?" I wanted to be a sassy pants—*Yes*, I could have replied and left it at that. But something told me that a woman who interrupted a perfect stranger's lunch on the way to the bathroom was not one to read social clues, subtle or otherwise. If I toyed with her, I would just be prolonging the awkward conversation.

"This one's a boy," I said.

"Congratulations," she repeated again and ambled off. A few minutes later, she returned from the powder room, and rather than going back to her own table, she hovered again at ours.

"Would you mind if I asked you a question?" she inquired. "Would you have kept trying if you found out this one was a girl?"

This woman's question seemed inappropriate on so many levels. I was at a restaurant. She was a stranger. I was licking French fry salt off of my thumb, and she was inquiring about our marital reproductive goals. She went on to explain how important she felt it was for a woman to "give her husband a son." In front of my two young daughters, she was saying that some moms wanted baby boys more than they wanted girls.

I had actually been psyched when I thought about having a third daughter. I could picture myself with a brood of girls. We would go horseback riding, line dancing, and star together in a remake of *Little Women*. In our later years, we would sing around the piano, play duets, and probably form some sort of quilting bee. Sure, most of my daydreams involved bucolic settings or activities more appropriate for the 1800s. But the point was, I knew girls. I already had two of them. We already had the blankets, the footie pajamas, and the hair bows. More than that, Ken and I had the girl know-how. We knew how to care for babies of that gender. When it came to a boy, well, that involved different equipment, a different maintenance plan. I was not all that keen to switch models after we had finally learned how to care for the female kind.

I wish I was the kind of person who could muster righteousness or stand and make speeches in a restaurant. I wish I was a person who could set aside my good manners when someone else failed to demonstrate her own. *Lady, get out of my privates*, I might have said. Or *What is this, 1980s China?* Instead, I stammered through something astonishingly clever like, "Gee, I never really thought about it." And then excused myself to the bathroom, half-afraid she would follow me back in there.

Interactions like these were not limited to hamburger eateries. Everywhere I went, if I admitted I was having a boy, heads nodded in approval. In the beginning, I thought folks were just cheering for us, hoping we could experience both kinds of children. My neighbor had five boys in a row and people were positively jubilant when she finally gave birth to a baby girl. But after months of overeager gender inquiries, I began to cringe at the implication. "You will finally get your boy," other mothers would cluck at family gatherings or after church, as though I had indicated a preference of one kind or another.

I came to resent the idea that my pregnancy was somehow more favorable since I was "giving my husband a son." It was sexist and old fashioned. I was a progressive woman with love in my heart for whatever child we got, whatever the name, whatever the gender, no matter how pregnant or not-pregnant people thought I looked. I found myself wondering, sometimes even hoping, that the sonogram folks had made a mistake. It would not have been our first incorrect baby prediction. When Katie was still in utero, her ultrasound photo session had been inconclusive. Every time the technician squirted that magic jelly on my belly and maneuvered the wand to broadcast an image, teeny Katie moved her hands like fig leaves to block a clear picture. We left the "gender reveal" appointment without any gender being revealed. The only definitive prediction of Katie's girlness—or boyness—had come on the doorstep of an inn in Cinque Terra, Italy. A gypsy woman offered to read my fortune. Before I could disagree, she dropped her keys on the ground. She was an older lady. Concerned she might injure her back, I bent down to retrieve them for her. As I did, she scrutinized my posture, put her hand on my tush, and declared, "*Mascolino!*" I offered a few coins and a smiling "*Grazie*" and went to bed thinking about Italian names that might sound good with the surname Harbaugh. (In case anyone is wondering, there are none. All male Italian names sound ridiculous with my husband's last name. Vincenzo Harbaugh, Liberato Harbaugh, Francesco Harbaugh . . . these are names for cartoon racecar drivers, not human sons.)

When our first daughter, Katherine Mary Harbaugh, came into this world, amid our confused joy, it never even occurred to me that the gypsy lady had ripped me off. Maybe her predictions were only 50 percent accurate. Or maybe she, like a preponderance of women I encountered during my pregnancies, assumed that what we were hoping to hear—and what we would pay more for—was knowledge that we were having a son. I prefer to believe that the old Italian woman was neither ineffectual nor malicious but rather ultraprescient. With her keychain trick and gentle butt caress, she had successfully predicted our *mascolino*, our baby boy swan song—her prediction was just seven and a half years too soon.

In the days before Henry's birth, I was conflicted about time. I both wanted to speed it up and make it stand still. I was sick of being pregnant, but I felt so blessed to have my two precious girls. Our family was already perfect. I cherished the quiet time with my first and second babies. While I was too large to have any lap left, I could still snuggle the girls on the couch or in my big bed. Propped on pillows, I would read to them or watch them sleep and brush golden locks of hair off of their foreheads. As I gazed at their faces, I was overwhelmed by the adventure and purpose at the core of being a parent. Days may have been stressful or tedious, but moments like these were gifts from God. I knew that once baby number three made his appearance, our little family would be topsy-turvy for a while. I saw that calm before the infant storm as a way to remind myself—and the girls—that we would be okay again soon.

As I gazed at their faces, I was overwhelmed by the adventure and purpose at the core of being a parent. Days may have been stressful or tedious, but moments like these were gifts from God.

 8 EVERY STORM ENDS

Eventually, pregnancy fatigue got the best of me, and we all grew tired of waiting for Henry. A week past my due date, our obstetrician sat me down and scheduled an induction. "Enough is enough," she said. "We need to help this baby come on out." I could not have agreed more. Two days later, Ken and I left the girls with my parents, and we headed for the hospital. It was Friday. Our son's birthday. I was ready.

Except, also, I wasn't. I had given birth to Katie and Lizzie naturally. No epidural. No drugs. Childbirth is a painful but fascinating process. My body had always coached me through it. I suspected this was my final pregnancy, and, suddenly, after all this time, I felt I was being cheated of the best part. I was being denied the all-natural labor I wanted. As a reasonable, college-educated woman, more than capable of self-advocating in difficult situations, I took a deep breath, opened my mouth to express these concerns to my doctor, and promptly began to cry.

"Can't we . . . just . . . wait [sniffle, sniffle] a few . . . more . . . days?" I sobbed. "Tomorrow . . . is . . . a . . . [sniffle] a . . . a . . . full . . . moon."

The doctor stared at me incredulously. The baby was more than a week late. I had needed assistance to climb onto the examination table. My baby "bump" extended to the top of my rib cage. I had worn the same dress to this appointment that I had worn two days prior because it was the only one that still fit. I had complained to absolutely everyone I knew about how miserable I was, how ready I was to be done, and now I was asking—begging, pleading—to be allowed to stay pregnant longer. Ken looked at me like I had just punched somebody. Then he closed his eyes, rubbed the bridge of his nose, and took a deep breath.

"Tell me what you need, Annmarie," he said. "Do you want me to be a consultant right now—someone to talk reason? Or a husband—someone to back you up?"

I glared at him. Did I want a business consultant in the room with me anticipating the birth of our first son? Uh, no. Obviously, I wanted a husband. He took my hand.

"Doc," he said, "I hear my wife saying she would like to wait. As her *husband*, I support this decision. What are our options?" Wearily, the doctor talked us through scenarios. If the baby was compromised in any way, we needed to induce today. Period. If not, well, she would think about it. She hooked me up to the fetal monitor, and after ascertaining that everything was all right with the baby in there—and probably just to get the hunormous wailing woman out of her office—she reluctantly agreed that we could wait another day or two.

"But if there's no baby this weekend, I want you in here Monday morning at seven," she said. "No more stalling." Ken and I left hand-in-hand, relieved. Now we could have the birth that we wanted.

We were idiots.

Not the Boss of Our Applesauce

Here's the thing about being veteran parents: we think we know everything. Because we've been through this baby business a time or two, we love to tell new parents how it is. We chuckle at their wipe warmers and decorative crib bumpers, forgetting that we once registered for those same frill items, believing them necessary. I have a friend who went to the hospital when her labor pains were three minutes apart, and the nurses sent her home because those supposed contractions were actually popcorn gas. That same friend nearly gave birth to her next child in the car because she waited so long to make sure she was really in labor. When it came to childbirth, by the third time around, Ken and I felt like old pros. We installed the infant car seat in the minivan and tossed our toothbrushes and a change of clothes in a grocery bag. We were ready to have another baby.

But what the husband, consultant, mother, and wife failed to consider was this: twice through anything does not mastery make. Pilots need more than two landings before they are cleared to fly airplanes. Actors need more than two rehearsals to get a play on its feet. And parents need more than two labors and deliveries before they can consider themselves experts on childbirth.

I know folks who will disagree vehemently with me on this topic. They will point to midwives and doulas and home births and water births and birth plans that specify acoustic guitar music and cord-cutting ceremonies and a professional photographer to capture images of the whole blessed mess. I am delighted for my friends and acquaintances who are able to have the birth experiences for which they choreograph and plan. But for every person who can point to labor and delivery utopia, I know dozens and dozens of others for whom that notion of the perfect birth just got in the way. Having a baby is a tricky business with life-and-death implications. There is no such thing as a perfect birth experience. There is only a birth experience. The perfect part is the baby at the end. By that point, you should count yourself lucky.

Ken and I left that hospital on a mission: we had two days to get this baby to come out. If it was described in childbirth folklore, we tried it: spicy food, sangria, foot massages, sexy time, raspberry tea, warm baths, sitting in a full yoga squat while breathing in the birth-inducing chi of the full moon. I do not know what, if anything, brought on the contractions. But late the next night, the first moment that I felt even the suggestion of a cramp, instead of resting, like I had when the girls were born, I got up and went downstairs, intent to let gravity do its thing. Unlike my prior childbirths, where contractions grew in intensity and frequency, this time, they were all over the map: three minutes apart, nine minutes apart, every two minutes for eight minutes, and then nothing at all for ten. They would not line up with any predictable regularity. But I wanted a natural delivery, so it was now or never. I remembered stories of friends who had walked the halls of the hospital, waiting for the baby to *drop*. I was determined to do the same here at home.

I called my brother, Kevin, who was on standby overnight babysitting duty. I told him it was not go time yet but that he should probably make sure he had gas in his car. Then I wandered around my house in the darkness. Ken and the girls were asleep, and I saw no need to wake anybody else until I was absolutely sure it was time. I walked small laps around the kitchen table and up and down the staircase to the living room. Then I unlocked the front door and went outside.

By the light of the full moon, I could see the magnolia tree was ready to bloom. Years ago, when the previous owners had landscaped, someone had envisaged that lovely southern tree as a good match for the northeastern Ohio snowbelt. Every year or two, that poor magnolia got snapped by a late freeze and dropped its buds like candy. But it was alive and ready that May. Already, a few of the topmost blossoms had begun to unfurl.

I paced the driveway and then took to the front sidewalk. The street was cold and quiet. I did not see any deer. Of course, they had already nibbled most of my garden tulips down to the nubbins, just as they did every spring. They would be back when the lilies tried to bloom. At least they left the daffodils alone. I stepped barefoot into the damp grass and stood for a moment before a struggling azalea bush. It had been dwarfed by hydrangeas that every year threatened to take over the front of the house, and the poor thing seemed to have barely survived the winter. I had been meaning to cut back the brown sticks of the hydrangeas to give the azalea a chance to survive. Well, there was no time like the present. I went to the garage and turned on the light. Ever the handyman, Ken had hung the rakes, shears, and shovels on the far side of the wall. I managed to squeeze behind his car, but—as I probably should have anticipated—I could not maneuver myself between the wall and the minivan in order to grab the tool I needed. I paused my quest for hedge clippers to time a contraction. It had been eight minutes since the last one. Plenty of time. I ambled into the house for my best kitchen shears and went back to the front yard. I lingered there in front of the azalea, timing another con- traction and paying a quiet moment of respect, not for this baby that was about to be but for the other one that never was. I began to trim.

Ken and I had planted the azalea only a year before, after a miscarriage had ended my pregnancy. It had been a difficult one from the beginning. We found out we were expecting a baby the same night my grandfather passed away. Most of the family was there at the old Kelly house by the train tracks, rotating in to say our goodbyes. I sat by my grandfather's bed, held his cool hand, and shared the news. He was the first person I told. Grandpa Kel was unconscious at the time, his breathing labored, his skin feathery and pale. Hospice had already been called in to keep him comfortable. If he kept my secret, I confided, maybe we would name the baby after him.

Grandpa Kel did keep the secret. He died early the next morning. Less than two months later, the baby died, too. At the time, I had thought maybe my body was telling me it was finished having babies. After all, I was not twenty-five anymore. I wasn't even thirty-five anymore. And yet, hardly a year later, there I was, standing barefoot in my front yard, pruning a hydrangea in the moonlight, about to have another child. I wanted to say something to mark the moment. I wished I was the kind of person who could quote scripture at will, who would know the exact right Biblical passage or even a bit of a poem to sum up the night. But it was just me and my azalea. There was no one else to take note or judge. I knelt down to touch its leaves, whispered, "Thank you," and went inside to wake up Ken.

.   .   .   .   .

The drive to the hospital was eerily calm. Unlike with Katie or Lizzie, I was not in extreme discomfort. The contractions were mild and infrequent. No water broke. We did not even valet the car. I walked from the parking lot to the emergency room carrying my own overnight bag on my shoulder.

Ask anyone who works in a hospital, and they will tell you that the full moon brings out the crazies. That night was no exception. There were two doctors on call in the maternity wing, and they had multiple women in labor all night long. Since I was still only four to five centimeters dilated upon arrival, I was encouraged to walk the halls. Rather than viewing this as a chore, I was heartened: at least the baby was coming. Because it was after midnight, the doors to the ward were locked, so I had access to only three small corridors. After the first few back-and-forth trips, I decided to proceed more deliberately. There were large poster prints hanging every ten or twenty feet. I paused before each painting to play

art critic during the contractions. After about twenty minutes, I decided that whoever had selected these pictures had done so haphazardly.
Perhaps they had been bundled in an interior designer's bulk discount
bin. There were depictions of farmhouses with confusing perspective
shifts and spring country scenes with entirely too much purple. Maybe
it was the contractions or impending labor, but painting after painting
confused me. Compositions were murky, storylines vague. I could not
understand the story being told in any of them. Until, tucked back in a
corner, I stood beneath *Blanco, Negro y Azul* by Carmen Galofré. During
this contraction, which felt stronger than the others, I looked at a line of
earthenware cups and pitchers on what appeared to be a simple table.
Most of the items were off-white, a few were charcoal; my eye was drawn
to one glass cup in the foreground that was blue. I had finally found a
work of art with a story, and the story turned out to be mine.

I had been worried about the effect of this boy on our already full
family. But, as the picture demonstrated, even at a crowded table, there
is always room for one more. I had been concerned about a boy when
we already had our two girls, but I could see the pleasing effect of the
three colors playing off of one another. There was no need to worry about
money. Our table would be simple, but we would be blessed with friends.
We would not put on airs. Our cups would be sturdy, not fragile. They
would likely not even be a matching set. But all would be welcome in this
family. All would be fed. I completed a few more hallway laps and kept
returning to the *White, Black, and Blue*. It was the last picture I looked
at before returning to my room. It turned out to be a fitting title for what
was about to come. It was time.

Except it was also time for everybody else.

I was only nine centimeters dilated, but I felt ready. The nurses set
up the room and detached the bottom of my bed, and during the next
contraction, my doctor indulged me one single push. In the next instant,
a nurse came running in saying a baby was "crowning" down the hall.
"Wait here," my doc said. "I'll be right back." I lay there with my legs in

the stirrups and did my best to relax. Ken played our Greatest Hits on his iPhone, and I breathed in the awful awesomeness of this moment. The back-up doc checked in, offering to deliver my baby, but I wanted to wait for the physician I knew. I felt relatively calm about a moment that was anything but.

I have only given birth to three children, but with each, I have been profoundly startled by the act of pushing. It is like no sensation I have ever experienced in any other context. It's like grabbing a knife, and when you realize it is cutting you, instead of letting go, you hold it tighter. And not with your hand, but with your private parts. There are very few instances when we journey toward pain then, upon experiencing it, walk even further in to discover something beautiful. I have failed at almost every other endeavor for which such a metaphor could apply: long-distance running, low-carb diets, high mountain hikes. But when it comes to babies, for a reason I don't entirely understand, my body escorts me through the pain.

When my doctor returned, I pushed for an hour, and that baby hardly budged. I wondered whether Henry had grown too big to be delivered naturally. My doctor assured me that was nonsense. I could do this. Another contraction came. I pushed briefly and immediately backed off. I changed my mind. This was too hard. "Come on, Annmarie. That was when you needed to bear down." She was urging me into the terrible pain. But I was tired, and I wanted her to shut up. I did not even push during the next contraction. I just skipped it and rested. "Are we doing this, or what?" she asked.

None of the things I said at that moment were very nice. But I knew what I had to do. During the next contraction, I pushed into the excruciating agony. When Ken saw the top of the baby's head, he mistakenly called out to me, "His head is out, Annmarie. You've done the hardest part." As he describes it, he was horrified when he realized that was only the very top of an enormous baby head. After the most difficult, painful push I have ever experienced, my baby got stuck. His shoulders were so big that to get him out, the nurses knelt on my pelvis to widen the opening. I did not so much push the baby out as lie there while an assortment of medical professionals went in there and grabbed him. As Ken tells the story, he heard the doctor shout and saw the delivery room fill with people in masks. I heard someone say, "Start timing." In my delirium, I thought they were timing contractions. Only later did I learn that Henry's crown had been dark purple and they were counting the seconds until the emergency C-section. When they paged a doctor to resuscitate, I assumed that person was for me. But she was on hand for my son.

Ken and I were foolish to have believed we knew best. We were never the boss of that applesauce.

6. You're Not the Boss of the Applesauce

We made all of the wrong decisions, but in the end, we were blessed. Henry arrived weighing ten pounds and three ounces, with the face of an angel and the body of a linebacker. We thought we knew best. We thought we were in charge. We thought if we just followed the path that we had in our minds, we would create our perfect birth experience. We were wrong. I felt as though I had been run over by a truck from the inside. As the painting's title had prophesied, I was white, black, and blue for many days to come. But even after all of the worry, stress, and fear, our cups have never been empty since Henry.

In the end, all it took was the better part of ten months, half a glass of sangria, a moonlight prayer, and the quick thinking of nine medical professionals to coax that baby out. Ken and I were foolish to have believed we knew best. We were never the boss of that applesauce. But Henry finally made his appearance. On the night of a full moon. Twelve days late. The storm of that pregnancy, labor, and delivery finally ended. We got our baby boy. And as Ken would tell you (if he felt like lying), I have hardly ever been crazy or overly sensitive since.

10: SEABIRD

I never really liked babies. I love my own, of course. But that's a genetic imperative. Other people's babies? For most of my adult life, my feelings ranged from mild disinterest to barely concealed annoyance. I never found their outfits particularly cute or their peek-a-boo games terribly entertaining. And traveling with them on airplanes? I would rather be stuck in the back-row middle seat next to the toilet than be sitting anywhere near someone else's baby in flight. Until, that is, the Philippines. In November of 2013, forty minutes after sunrise, in the wake of the worst typhoon in recorded human history, I changed my mind about kids.

A few months earlier, I never imagined I would soon be halfway around the world dealing with the aftermath of an epic natural disaster. I had a good job making lives better for military vets. I had enough on-the-side adventures with my kids. And I had a family that seemed content, close to our Ohio relatives and with a tight circle of friends. Then a chance conversation with two former Marines changed everything.

Jake Wood and Will McNulty approached me at a conference for veterans with a proposal.

"We're about to change the world," Will said. "Care to join us?"

Their young nonprofit, Team Rubicon, was growing quickly. I had followed its progress ever since the mission to Haiti in 2010. In fact, The Mission Continues, the nonprofit I helped found, awarded Jake a fellowship early on. Since then, Team Rubicon had blossomed into thousands of veterans and first responders standing by to help whenever disaster struck. Their reputation was growing just as fast. The idea, to repurpose veterans' skills for redeployment to disaster zones, was working. What started as an impulsive mission to help the people of Haiti was becoming a phenomenon.

So when the question came, I was intrigued.

"Change the world?" I said. "What do you have in mind?"

The request was simple. Quit my job, drop everything, move to Los Angeles, and grow a staff of ten into an organization that could lead a global movement to not only change the face of disaster relief but transform a generation of veterans.

Inside, I knew my answer had to be "yes," but I had learned a thing or two in fifteen years of marriage. So I said, "Let me think about it . . . and call my wife." I phoned Annmarie as soon as I got back to the hotel room.

"I want to do this," I said. "I have been submitting policy proposals about giving veterans a sense of purpose. I have been advocating in DC for ideas that *might* make something happen. These guys . . . they are doing it. They're making real everything I've been talking about."

"Well," she said, "it's just in time."

"For what?" I said.

"You're thirty-nine. Half of your friends have started their midlife crises. They're asking themselves what their lives are about, and they're out spending money on BMWs—or worse—as a way to avoid answering that."

"I don't need a BMW," I said. "A girlfriend, maybe . . ."

"Listen," she said, ignoring my attempt at humor, "I get it. This job is *exactly* what you were made to do. It's on the front lines. It has real and immediate impact. It needs someone with your experience with vets and your willingness to take risks. I don't think anyone else can do it. I'd pick this over a midlife crisis any day. We just have to figure out the rest."

"So we're in?" I asked.

"We're in."

It is a rare thing to be surrounded, every day, by people you admire. That is the position I found myself in late in 2013 when I accepted the job as Chief Operations Officer for Team Rubicon. It was a tiny team with big plans. When they said they intended to change the world, they—we—meant it. I set off for Los Angeles with whatever I could cram in the back of my thirty-year-old station wagon. Annmarie and the kids stayed in Ohio on the promise that I would fly home as often as possible. Eventually, we would have to figure out something more permanent. As I drove away, all we knew for certain was that this job mattered and that I felt called to do it. But it still felt discouraging to leave my family behind yet again.

As bad luck would have it, a major flood struck a Colorado mountain town as I prepared to leave. This was not a normal flash flood but a once-every-five-hundred-years event. Days earlier, a forest fire had scarred the upriver mountainside, leaving the terrain baked hard and unable to soak up moisture. Then a massive storm dumped so much rain that the waterways swelled and ran together. In three short hours, the lazy St. Vrain Creek, which a toddler could normally wade across, grew into a twenty-five-foot-deep monster.

I adjusted my route and headed to join the relief effort. Team Rubicon's response was already in full swing with a forward operating base (FOB) set up in a Home Depot parking lot. Each morning, strike teams suited up in their iconic grey t-shirts. Many talked with pride about trading one uniform for another, about discovering a renewed sense of purpose as a Team Rubicon *greyshirt*. We loaded our trucks with gear then set out for a full day's work. The simplicity of the labor itself belied the complexity of the operation. The command center at the

FOB operated nearly round the clock, collecting damage assessments from field teams, assigning work orders, and managing volunteers who showed up to help. I spent my first few days mucking out homes: filling wheelbarrows shovel by shovel and digging through mud and debris that in some houses was piled four feet deep. On day three, my secret slipped out—I was the incoming COO for Team Rubicon. I got reassigned to ride shotgun with one of our field leaders so that I could better observe the challenges of running an operation this size.

I was awestruck by what I saw—how a tiny creek could become a raging torrent in a matter of hours. We came to a washed-out section of road with water still cutting through it. A hundred yards beyond was a bridge, which spanned nothing but the former riverbed, now dry. In one evening, the creek had carved a new course, oblivious to the fact that a community had been built along it. Roads and bridges, houses and schools, all had been planned around where people assumed their river would always be. In a single terrifying night, the river changed its mind.

As struck as I was by the force of nature's fury, I was more impressed by the men and women of Team Rubicon. Greyshirt volunteers had taken time off their regular jobs to stare down this flood, to help its victims on the worst days of their lives. We came upon one elderly man whose home was inundated. This particular job was a big one—mud three feet deep throughout his kitchen and bedroom. One bucket at a time, Team Rubicon helped reclaim his home. The volunteers took great care, uncovering valuables and photos and setting them aside like they were their own. I noticed one black-and-white photo of the old man in uniform standing by a plane.

Greyshirt volunteers had taken time off their regular jobs to stare down this flood, to help its victims on the worst days of their lives.

"Is that a B-17?" I asked him.

It was. The man was a veteran, a B-17 gunner in WWII. He fought

5 | Talk to Strangers

in the same war as my grandfather, flying in the same type of aircraft my grandpa had piloted. When I told the man that the team helping him was made up of veterans, he broke down. He told me that the last time he had been this proud of his country was when the US Army liberated his POW camp in Germany.

When it comes to finding purpose, there is no better way than helping others in the aftermath of a disaster. Every night at our FOB, we cracked open a few beers and shared stories of the day behind us: the destroyed homes, the heartbroken families, the communities still reeling. But we also forged new bonds, the type of bonds I had not felt since leading crews as a combat recon pilot in the Navy. For many of the greyshirts gathered in that Home Depot parking lot, Team Rubicon became family.

Within a year of my first mission, I saw the organization break new ground, defying the expectations of everyone except those who understood what vets are capable of. Team Rubicon was rated among the top ten nonprofits in America to work for (Hrywna 2016). Today, there are more than thirty-five thousand members, standing by to deploy whenever disaster strikes. It has conducted over 150 missions, responding to earthquakes, wildfires, floods, tornadoes, and typhoons. New chapters are now launching in other countries, with military veterans from Australia, the United Kingdom, and Germany being given the chance to apply their skills and training in disaster zones around the globe.

One operation in particular captured the spirit of this incredible organization. Operation Seabird, our response to Typhoon Haiyan in the Philippines, demonstrated what veterans can accomplish in the midst of chaos.

SUNRISE

Typhoon Haiyan remains one of the largest storms in recorded history. When it made landfall in November of 2013, it brought sustained winds of 196 miles per hour and gusts topping 250. Had it hit the United States, its outer bands would have stretched from Washington, DC, to

Los Angeles, CA. I flew into the disaster zone with Team Rubicon's initial wave, arriving on one of the first Marine Corps C-130s carrying relief workers. My team landed on a pitch-black runway in a city with no lights. Amidst the rubble of a military barracks, we established our FOB. Being among the first relief organizations on the ground, we picked a spot right next to the helicopter pads. It gave us the best chance for catching flights into the stricken outlying villages, but it also meant we had to hold down our tents every time the helos took off.

The next morning, at first light, we boarded one of those Philippine Air Force Hueys and headed south. What we saw confirmed our worst fears. Nothing was left intact. Even the sturdiest buildings had their roofs ripped away. The storm surge had rushed for miles, reducing houses to matchsticks. Ships lay hundreds of yards inland, like toys dropped amid the debris. I have been in warzones. But nothing compared to the devastation I saw flying along the Philippine coastline.

We circled the village of Tanauan and identified what we assumed was the clinic. Between the scattered rubble and crowds of people, there was no way to land. So we diverted to a strip of empty beach a few miles away. As we approached, people sprinted toward the descending helicopter. The pilot hovered a few feet off the ground, and we leapt. As our ride lifted away, a crowd of villagers gathered. We had been warned that they might try to take our supplies. The opposite was true. They were hungry and scared, but grateful, and they helped us make our way to the clinic.

The makeshift hospital was set up inside the former city hall, one of the only buildings left with walls still standing. Hundreds were already gathered, seeking medical help. Most had walked miles. The floor was covered in waste, wounds were starting to fester, and the air stank of gangrene. I made my way to the second floor where a surgery was underway.

The operating theater was an old office, and a patient lay on two desks shoved together and covered with clear plastic. Surgeons crouched under a blue tarp held up by bits of string. Rain from the last monsoon downpour still dripped onto them. The lead doctor turned to me with bloody hands and said, "Drop your gear and sterilize these instruments. I hope to God you brought antibiotics." As an afterthought, he added, "And hide your food." Immediately, our team of fourteen greyshirts set about tending to the injured and stabilizing the building. Our engineers climbed on the roof to secure sturdier tarping so the surgeons could work without getting soaked. Our logisticians passed critical details back to the FOB, relaying types of injuries we encountered and the treatments and medications we needed more of. And our linguist provided an essential link between the docs and the masses of patients who could not speak English.

All day and all night, patients arrived in a steady stream, bearing gaping, jagged gashes, many of them showing signs of gangrene. For a rookie like me, those injuries were at least straightforward. Open, clean, disinfect, pack, and bandage. That I could handle.

The "injury" that knocked me off balance, oddly enough, had nothing to do with the typhoon. Late one evening, a pregnant woman arrived on the back of a moped. She was in labor, but struggling. The clinic was blacked out, lit only by the occasional flashlight and our headlamps bobbing up and down as we worked. Patients lay huddled in groups on the floor. Our OBGYN led the expectant mother to the "operating table" and immediately determined a normal delivery was out of the question because of how the baby was positioned. A C-section would be necessary to save the lives of both mother and child.

With no power, we did not have enough light to perform the procedure at night. Even with everyone's headlamps focused on the incision point, the surgeon deemed it too risky. So the team chose the one course of action in the midst of crisis that is sometimes most difficult of all: *nothing*. All night, we waited. For eight hours, we took turns comforting this woman, praying that the earth might turn faster and daylight might end her ordeal. Team members wiped her brow and applied counter pressure to her hips and back. During a break, I tried to doze but woke to the sound of the woman crying out in pain.

When the first ray of sun split the horizon, I said a prayer. *Please help this mother. Please save this baby.* Within twenty minutes, there was adequate light to begin prep. She would need so much anesthetic that we would have to ration it for the rest of our patients. Wound cleanings from then on would have to be done with little or no pain relief. I did not care—I just wanted this mother and child to make it.

As the surgery began, a few of us huddled on the floor around a camp stove. Someone brewed a pot of tea, and we sat in silence, sipping from tin mugs, straining to hear the doctors talking softly to each other as they worked. Then a sound I will never forget: a baby's cry, healthy, strong, and defiant.

I felt the sun warming my neck, looked down into my cup, and wept. I tried to make my tears less obvious. My team in the Philippines included some of the toughest people I have ever known: combat medics, Special Forces operators, a paratrooper from the French Foreign Legion. When I looked up, I could see we all felt the same thing—our faces wore identical expressions of exhaustion and relief, but above all—joy. That baby may have been crying the loudest, but we all joined in varying degrees.

When I am out on a mission, I usually try not to think about my family. During my Navy deployments or my time in Afghanistan, I found it easier to stay focused on the job if I did not dwell on thoughts of home. But that morning, with a brand new baby declaring loudly to the world that she wanted to live, I could not help but think of my own children, of each of their births and how incredibly lucky I was. Lizzie, with all of her health issues, had the best medical care in the world. Henry, whose birth was so difficult, had a fully equipped operating theater and an army of doctors and nurses to deal with any eventuality. Bringing my three kids into the world was nerve wracking every time. But my experience in the Philippines, witnessing the delivery of a child in a disaster zone with only the morning sun as our light, gave me new perspective on the meaning of *blessed.*

Six hours after that sunrise, we called in a Philippine Air Force helicopter to evacuate our most critical patients. A cardiac case, an amputee, a new mother, and a six-hour-old baby girl were airlifted to Manila. Miracles do happen. Even in the wake of tragedy. To this day, whenever I hear a baby cry, I smile inside. Even on airplanes.

SEABIRD

When I described to Annmarie later what a typhoon is like, I used the term "meat grinder." It is not just the wind that causes damage but the tidal surge. In some places, it reached twenty feet deep, rushing inland, tearing down everything in its path. Jagged tin roofing, splintered wooden beams, crushed cars, and people churned together. Most victims drowned. But those who survived the wind and water were left stranded and sometimes gravely injured. The meat grinder effect resulted in gruesome injuries: amputations, crush wounds, deep gashes embedded with debris. In the aftermath of such a storm, wells are contaminated, sewage runs through the streets, and bodies are strewn everywhere. It is impossible to keep wounds dry, much less clean.

So when a father came into our clinic carrying his daughter, foot bandaged, I feared the worst. She was Katie's age. My gaze met the dad's, and I instantly recognized the look in his eyes—that tortured mix of love and terror only a parent knows. We unwrapped the strips of clothing around the girl's leg. As each layer came off, the stench of gangrene grew stronger. Dad held his daughter's hand tightly while they listened to the surgeon's words.

"We will probably have to cut off her foot," the doctor said. "Do you understand?"

It was swollen to the size of a melon, a five-inch gash from heel to toe oozing white pus. There was no way to know how deep the infection went until we opened and cleaned the wound. But there could be no misunderstanding about what was likely to happen. The father nodded, squeezing his daughter's hand tighter. "We understand," he said through our translator.

Over the next few days, I lost count of the number of patients we treated. With no medical charts to track wound care, our doctors wrote instructions with Sharpie markers directly onto the patients' skin. An infected leg, cleaned and wrapped, would have the date of treatment, medications administered, and instructions for re-dressing: *12 Nov, 10 mg morphine, clean/change daily.* We hoped against hope that everyone leaving our clinic could keep their wounds clean and dry. Sometimes, infection and injury won out, and an amputation resulted. Other times, we got lucky. That little girl did not lose her foot.

When our supplies dwindled, we handed off to another relief team. The drive back to the airfield took hours, giving us a close-up view of what we had flown over—bodies stacked like cordwood, homes smashed to bits, and thousands making their way toward the main airfield. We arrived at our FOB to find it overwhelmed by refugees seeking a way out.

As much as I tried to focus on the job, everywhere I looked, I saw things that reminded me of my own kids. I saw children, newly orphaned, huddling inside empty body bags to stay dry as the monsoon rains poured down. I saw a father lift his son over a chain-link fence into the arms of a soldier, begging for a single spot on the transport plane about to leave. When I heard someone mention the date, I realized it was Annmarie's birthday. I dialed home on one of our satellite phones and sang "Happy Birthday" to her voicemail. I hung up then got my head back in the game.

Two weeks after the storm made landfall, a significant influx of aid was finally beginning to arrive. We divided our team. Our medics settled into a rotation staffing the airfield clinic, while assessment teams pushed out to determine where the most critical relief needs were. I joined one of those teams to deliver two pallets of food aid via a US Marine Corps Osprey to an outlying community. We overflew the village and spotted an open cane field a few miles south. The pilots signaled back to me. I told my team to memorize the rendezvous point and prepare to offload. The aircraft needed to refuel and pick up more food, but we would be back in exactly eight hours at this same spot.

The Osprey touched down, and we began to unload the pallets. Within minutes, a crowd of nearly four hundred had gathered. We had food for maybe half that number. As the Osprey lifted off, I looked down through the open rear ramp. My team of four, wearing their bright red Team Rubicon helmets, was swarmed by hundreds of desperately hungry villagers.

The aircraft headed west, toward the refueling point a hundred miles away. The damage on that side of the island was minor compared to what the eastern half had endured. Palm trees were stripped bare and roofs were mangled, but most structures had survived. We landed, and the pilots requested fuel and additional relief supplies. Among the foreign workers manning the aid effort, there was a lack of urgency I found infuriating. Perhaps it was because they had not seen the full scale of the disaster. Perhaps it was because they were in someone else's country. In any case, we waited the entire day to refuel, and by the time we were ready to take off, dusk was upon us.

The pilots received an order to return to the main airfield so their food pallets could be added to the massive pile awaiting distribution. It was a clear example of bureaucracy getting in the way of meaningful help. I leveled with them. "You saw what I saw," I said. "There are people who need that food *right now*, and I've got a team that needs to be picked up—they are counting on us to be there." It was not much of an argument. I was a former naval aviator, they were Marine pilots, and we spoke the same language. They made a beeline for the rendezvous point; we offloaded the pallets and picked up my team. I don't know if those pilots got in trouble, but I doubt it. In a disaster, you have to call the play as it happens. Like parents, Marines get that better than anyone.

Every storm ends. Three weeks after the typhoon, the main airfield was finally operating with some semblance of a plan. Aid came in; evacuees got out. A new wave of Team Rubicon greyshirts arrived to relieve us, and it was time for us to go. We loaded ourselves into a US Air Force

Three weeks after the typhoon, the main airfield was finally operating with some semblance of a plan. Aid came in; evacuees got out. A new wave of Team Rubicon greyshirts arrived to relieve us, and it was time for us to go.

8 · EVERY STORM ENDS

C-130 bound for Manila. The plane was already packed to capacity with civilian evacuees. The only remaining space was on the tail ramp. We clung to the pallet tracks as the ramp lifted off the tarmac and sealed the plane shut. Most of us were asleep before we left the ground.

Twenty-four hours later, we boarded a commercial flight back to the US. A folded blanket lay on my seat, and a flight attendant asked if I needed anything. It was jarring, like coming home from Afghanistan. I began to process what I had seen. Our plane taxied onto the runway. As its engines roared, I buried my face in the airline blanket, pressed it against the window, and wept until I ran out of breath.

It took months before I was able to talk about my time in the Philippines. I started slowly, telling Annmarie about the team, about the bond we had formed. Katie, I knew, wanted to ask me about it, too. I was still flying back and forth from Cleveland to LA, and I wanted her to realize why this job was so important. I wanted her to understand my passion for vets and for victims of disaster. Most of all, I wanted her to know why my work took me away from her.

One evening, after a fresh snowfall had blanketed the streets, Katie and I went for a walk. We headed downtown toward the ice cream shop (it's always ice cream weather in the Harbaugh house). Ours were the first footprints in the snow. As our feet crunched down the sidewalk, I told Katie about the clinic in the Philippines. I told her about the girl her age, about how the doctors had saved the infected foot, and about how brave she had been through it all. Katie stayed quiet for a long time. We talked about other things, too. But I could tell her mind was somewhere else.

On the way home, we retraced our steps. She put her arm around my waist and said, "I'm glad you told me, Dad, about the girl."

"I wanted you to know, sweetheart," I said. "I wanted to explain why I leave you and Lizzie and Henry."

"Oh," she answered, "I already know why you go. I just knew something was bothering you, and I wanted you to be able to talk about it."

I almost stopped, but I didn't want Katie to see me tear up. She sensed it and pulled closer to me.

"I brag about you all the time, Dad," she said. "I miss you, but I'm really proud of you, and you don't have to explain anything to me."

At times, Katie can seem like the most self-involved kid in the world. She spends an unusual amount of time brushing her hair. She likes the trinkets on her desk arranged just so. And after her last birthday, she complained when the pillowcase I bought her was aqua instead of teal. Yet Katie realized *I* was the one who needed this walk. I had set out intending to share some fatherly wisdom, to give her strength for the times we were apart. But kids are braver than we think. Whatever wisdom passed on that walk was entirely from her to me.

11: Single Married Mother of Three

I have been told that having children is a bit like joining the Marine Corps. It breaks you down. You lose your hair, your dignity, and the chance to go to the bathroom whenever you feel like it.

Unlike joining the Marines, however, having kids does not also build you back up into some well-trained, physically fit version of yourself. Instead, living with children is like perpetual Basic Training. There is yelling. The food isn't very good. Everything hurts. And you never, ever get to sleep in.

I have also heard that having children is like joining the circus. There is a lot of poop to contend with. The chairs are often sticky. Crunchy snacks are forever on the floor. And though there are no elephants, transporting a family via minivan is a lot like driving a car full of clowns.

I have been to the big top, and I know lots of veterans. These analogies are pretty close. But I think it is more accurate to say that having children is like joining a Marine Corps run exclusively by clowns. Or like attending a circus put on by Marines. As parents, we know that this business of raising kids is really important stuff, but some days, a lot of days, it feels absolutely ridiculous.

First as a consultant, and later, at Team Rubicon, Ken was typically away Monday through Friday. He missed five out of every seven bedtimes and fifteen out of every twenty-one meals. He was seldom around to pack lunches, fold laundry, or sit for twenty interminable minutes in the elementary school pick-up line. He missed birthdays, recitals, and the father-daughter craft night at Lizzie's school.

Without him, I fought the good fight. With coffee and cable television, I powered through. But I was bedraggled, bone tired, and bushwhacked caring for our three children alone. By about 4:45 most afternoons, I was ready to kick everyone, including me, into bed. I was supposed to be a freelance writer, but I pitched pieces I never wrote and joined workshops I never attended. When I wasn't exhausted, I was lonely, and when I wasn't lonely, I was mad. I missed the company of people over the age of eight. I chatted incessantly with grocery clerks and gas station attendants, fishing for adult conversation. With the exception of shoveling snow, I never left the house without my children. We were together all the time. Most nights, when we made it to actual bedtime, I read the kids a few pages of *Harry Potter* or *Junie B. Jones* and fell asleep on their bedroom floor. Occasionally, I would stumble downstairs to watch *The Daily Show* over a bowl of ice cream. But I did not write. How could I write about parenting when I was so busy *being a parent*?

One night, as I roasted my third s'more over a gas burner in the kitchen, it occurred to me that I needed some help. I am not a person who enjoys asking for assistance. I like to show folks I can handle my business. I want to be that put-together woman in church whose children are well mannered and impeccably groomed. Except I had been wearing the same yoga pants for four days and my kids had spent most of a recent church sermon shouting the word *unicorn*. I could no longer recall the last time I blow-dried my hair, and I was now preparing campfire food inside my home—by myself. It was time to call for reinforcements.

Unlike the circus or the Marine Corps, when it comes to parenthood, it behooves you to escape. Go AWOL. Abandon your post. Change your socks. My parents were happy to sweep in and take charge of my children. The kids adored Nonna and Pops and loved their homemade chicken soup, games of freeze tag, and outings to the library, bookstore, and park. My siblings chipped in, too. Uncle Kevin and Auntie Alex took the kids for ice cream or a movie. Auntie Jenny and Uncle Scott hosted sleepovers and babysat. My other brother, John, and his wife, Rose, checked in frequently to see if I needed coffee or adult company at the end of a long day—114 percent of the time, the answer was a resounding YES. Without the love and support of my family, Ken's prolonged absences would have been more than I could bear.

When it comes to parenthood, it behooves you to escape. Go AWOL. Abandon your post.

7 CHANGE YOUR SOCKS

But every family has a taker, the member who asks for far more than she gives. The mooch. I did not want to be the one constantly leaning on the Kelly clan for favors and assistance. Except single-parenting was breaking me. Though I had not drafted a budget since high school economics—thanks, Mr. Tomaskovich!—I sat the kids down in front of *Tom and Jerry* one afternoon and reconfigured my life. After eliminating Starbucks, refinancing the minivan, and canceling my fancy gym membership (when was the last time I had even gone there?), I hired some babysitters. I refused to be one of those moms sitting home with my s'mores, getting angrier and angrier at my husband *about a life that we had chosen together*. Despite the pay cut he was taking, I supported Ken's transition out of the corporate world. I had insisted he give Team Rubicon a chance. I wanted him to find happiness. I simply had not considered the toll that his pursuit of happiness would take on mine.

From then on, I quit bellyaching and stopped making excuses. If I really wanted to do something, I did it. If I wanted to go somewhere, I went. I bought a single ticket for a Cleveland author series and heard

David Sedaris read from his new book. I attended plays and concerts. I volunteered at church and met friends for coffee. I sold an essay to National Public Radio and drove into the city to record it. And most of all, despite my penchant for reruns of *How I Met Your Mother*, I forced myself to write every day, even if most of it was useless drivel and over-wrought nonsense that no one ever read but me. I stopped letting the fact that I was a single mom 71.4 percent of the time suffocate me. I changed my socks.

I spent a small fortune on babysitters (Nicole and Mary Kate—you gals were the best!) and made the most of this long-distance marriage business. Whenever he flew back from LA, Ken took over parenting duties most Saturdays so I could sleep, exercise, and write. He worked hard to provide for our family, and I had the strength and support of our Chagrin Falls community. Weeks were long, but we knew the saying about absence making the heart grow fonder. We probably could have continued relatively happily in our balanced imbalance had it not been for two small incidents. The first was Halloween.

> *We probably could have continued relatively happily in our balanced imbalance had it not been for two small incidents.*

 **4 IMBALANCE IS BALANCE**

JIMMY BUFFETT AND THE HEADLESS HORSEMAN

We had been living in Chagrin Falls for three years, and after stints in Florida, South Carolina, and Virginia, I never tired of the change of seasons in Northeastern Ohio—the way winter's first freeze surprised us every year, how crocuses relentlessly battled snowflakes each spring, and the tentative feel of the sun when the swimming pool opened in June. But fall—fall was the best. Autumn meant the Geauga County Fair, the Apple Butter Festival, farm-to-table dinners, and donning a jacket at the high school football games. And, of course, Halloween.

Our last Halloween in Chagrin Falls was glorious. For once, Ken was home, and our little family celebrated the holiday together. The air was sweet with mulled cider and toasted pumpkin seeds, and we could hear kids screaming at the Haunted Fire House in town. Leaves crunched beneath our feet as we ambled from one tailgate party to another. Our neighbors and friends gave us hot dogs, candy apples, and Great Lakes Brewing Company pumpkin ale. It was a swell night.

Later that evening, after the kids had sugar-crashed into sleep, Ken and I sat in front of a fire and watched a bootleg copy of Disney's 1949 *The Legend of Sleepy Hollow* while we raided the kids' candy stashes. I filched a Snickers bar from Henry's pail and reflected back on the night. "That was fun," I said, a string of caramel clinging to my bottom lip.

"Yeah," Ken said, gently brushing the goop off my mouth. "You sure do have a lot of friends. You know half the town."

"Correction," I said, scouring Lizzie's bucket for a Twix bar. "*We* know half the town."

"No," Ken said firmly. "*You.*" I tried to correct him again, but he continued. "Before tonight, I had never met most of those people."

"That's not true," I tried to interject. "You met them last spring at the Easter egg hunt."

"No," he replied. "I missed that. Tonight, when the guy in the Jimmy Buffett shirt walked up and gave me a beer, I thought he was just an eccentric trick-or-treater. I didn't know he was Sherry's husband. And truthfully, even after he introduced himself, I was still thinking, *Who the heck is Sherry?*"

"Oh, you know Sherry. She runs the—"

"That's not my point," Ken said. "You have a lot of friends here. I don't." I thought about what he had said and conceded it was probably true.

"But I've never known many of your work friends," I said.

"Work friends?" said Ken. "At the firm, we were based in twenty different cities every week. I knew a couple of the guys, but it's not like we hung out. I had colleagues, and I had clients."

"What about Team Rubicon?" I asked. "Is it different there?"

"TR is special," he replied. "They are a great bunch of people. I would like you to get to know them some day."

My husband was away every week. He got to fly to exotic cities and watch movies in comfortable hotel rooms. When he was a consultant, he could order room service on the company tab. I had always focused on the sacrifices *I* was making—caring for the children full time, cleaning up vomit when they had the flu, packing all those freakin' school lunches, putting my career on hold. I had never given much thought to the sacrifice *he* was making. He no longer played on his club soccer team or spent time with the guys watching the Super Bowl. He was away too much to be an active member of the Dads' Club, the Jaycees, or even the local American Legion post. And he was missing the kids' childhoods. Henry had taken his first steps while Ken was in Tampa. Katie had danced in *Alice in Wonderland* while Ken was in San Francisco. Lizzie had attended her school's father-daughter night with me; we built a birdhouse that we hung in the backyard. Sure, Ken was making an effort to get home most weekends, but he was still missing too much. And he was lonely. He probably had been for quite some time, but I had never noticed.

We watched Ichabod Crane's demise in silence. One night, after a holiday party, Ichabod disappeared. Had Mr. Crane, who had been a nervous teacher in Sleepy Hollow, really just moved on to another town? Maybe. Or had the Headless Horseman gotten him? Walt Disney and Washington Irving left it to us to imagine Ichabod's fate. Though it had been one of my favorite stories as a child, as an adult, I disliked how *The Legend of Sleepy Hollow* ended. Halloween or not, this was just one more cautionary tale that taught us to fear the darkness, to avoid uncharted waters, and to hover indoors rather than walk in the light of the moon.

Soon after, we drifted upstairs to sleep, and the next morning, Ken was off again—before I even woke up. Usually, he headed back to the office in LA, but not always. Sometimes, there were fundraising trips or disaster operations to study and improve. Usually, I did not even bother to ask where he was heading. It made no difference. I just knew he would not be home. The kids and I resumed our daily routine of bus stops and homework, baths, and babysitters. We were too busy to miss Dad all that much. Though I could not help but think about how much he seemed to miss us.

A few weeks later, I found myself feeling his absence more deeply.

Jane Eyre Never Went There

I was driving home from a meeting of our family book club. My mother had given each of her four children a hardbound copy of *To Kill a Mockingbird* the previous Christmas and inscribed the books in her infamous calligraphy script. Mom took a penmanship course in the late '80s and has the best handwriting I have seen this side of the Industrial Revolution. Her note read: *The one thing I ask of my children is that you read my favorite book and gather with me to discuss this timeless work of literature.*

Mom had surely not meant for her message to be ironic, but it was. Our mother requested all sorts of things from us all of the time: "Read this email about angels and send it to five people you know." "Come to your cousin's mother-in-law's funeral. You know it would mean a lot to her." "Next time you are home, would you please take a look at the computer monitor? It's doing that thing with the virus update again, and I don't know whether or not to click OK." Mom did not know how *not* to ask us things.

To be fair, however, we asked a lot of our mother, too. She attended my kids' basketball games and recitals and babysat any time I asked, including the longer stints with Katie when Lizzie was hospitalized. She did our laundry whenever she visited, cooked homemade soup just because, and showered the kids with gifts at every opportunity, from Arbor Day to Hanukkah. She hosted all the family dinners and planned all the birthday celebrations and always had time to attend my Dad's choir concerts or feed my sister's cat. And even though my brothers are gainfully employed grown men, Mom still cuts their hair. What can I say? She could not stop being a mom if she wanted to.

And so, when Mom asked us to do something, we did it. We formed a Family Book Club and gathered every month or two to discuss a great work of literature. *For Mom.* We began, as requested, with *To Kill a Mockingbird.* Though I had taught the novel to high school students a half dozen times, I had never discussed the text with my family. At first, it was a bit awkward engaging in quasi-academic conversation when we were more accustomed to chitchat and making fun of each other. Even though we talked all the time, we were not sure how to talk to each other in a book club. We danced around the story's usual themes—racism, sexism, how the wisdom of children is often overlooked by adults who presume to know better.

But it was not until we turned to Boo Radley that we hit our stride. We were reminiscing about the Boo Radleys we had grown up with, the fixtures in our own neighborhoods that we had been in awe of or feared. A few of us remembered the old lady down the hill who yelled at us for picking her daffodils and our neighbor, Mrs. Swain, who just yelled, period. My mom told of Taduccio, an old man who would holler at the neighborhood kids from his front porch down the hill. My father, who had grown up one of ten children, claimed not to have any shut-ins or mysterious figures living nearby. "It was just a normal family neighborhood," he said. "There was nobody terribly odd or unusual." Then he thought for a minute and said, "Unless you mean old Hungy Joe." *Hungy,* we learned, had been short for Hungarian, and the fellow lived in a small shack by the railroad tracks. He spoke very little English, and when the children would sneak over to take a look in his cabin, he would run them off with a shovel. "Yeah, Dad," we said. "Hungy Joe counts." We talked about what role these outsiders had played in our childhoods, the stories kids had told, the rumors. It was delightful to be children in a room with our parents, listening to them imagine themselves being children again. We were finally peers. Family Book Club put us on an equal playing field.

More books followed, as did more moments of family intimacy and more breaks with tradition. For *The Great Gatsby*, my mom and dad arrived dressed as Daisy and Gatsby—Mom in a flowing white gown and Dad in a dapper vest, white trousers, and a cap. I had never seen my father don anything remotely like a costume, unless you counted the green hoodie he wore when our high school tennis matches lasted past sunset. Gatsby encouraged my parents to be romantic and playful. Dad was less enthusiastic about *Pride and Prejudice*, our next read. "I never read it before, and now that I have, I feel confident I will never read it again," he remarked. Most of the fellows in the room, in fact, had been less than enthralled with the book I had considered my favorite through most of my late teens. It was odd to realize that something I loved did not elicit the same response in my family.

When my sister chose *Jane Eyre* to follow, I tried not to roll my eyes. If Dad did not like *Pride and Prejudice*, *Jane Eyre* would be no better. I had read it in high school and again in college but never really liked it all that much myself. I had no use for literary characters whose lives were a shambles unless they were falling apart in an interesting way—a torrid love affair, a confrontation between good and evil. Jane struck me as humorless, simultaneously timid and stubborn, and someone who might have been more in control of her own destiny had she not been so worried about what others thought. Even her love affair bored me. Unlike Elizabeth Bennett, whom I considered my literary BFF, Jane Eyre was wearisome. I was half-tempted not to even bother reading the book again. But I wanted to be a good sport, so I puttered through the lengthy tome. And I am glad that I did. It is said that for a work of literature to be deemed a "classic," it must elicit a new response in us each time we read it. *Jane Eyre* is such a book. Rereading it as an adult, I was struck by the feminism of the text, its forward thinking. Jane made a choice to live

apart from the man she loved. She possessed honor, strength, a quiet dignity, and a willingness to sacrifice her own happiness for that of another
person. Instead of the mousy orphan I remembered, Jane seemed quite
independent, even brave. I realized I could learn a thing or two from this
young woman.

During my drive home from Family Book Club, I heard a portion of
a public radio discussion about single moms. I have no beef with single
parents. After working with teenagers most of my teaching career, I keep
in touch with a dozen or so former students who are raising children on
their own. They are proud, hardworking young ladies. And knowing full
well how difficult parenting is, I respect my former students' tenacity
and devotion to their children. But it was the children of single moms
upon which the radio program focused. Specifically, the daughters. The
researcher being interviewed explained that a high percentage of girls
raised by single moms also become pregnant at a young age. Daughters
of single moms are more likely to become single mothers themselves.

I almost flipped the channel right then. Here was another thinly
veiled attack on single parents. Surely young girls raised by strong, independent mothers would learn a similar strength and self-worth. I felt
like calling the radio station to ask when they would be airing a program
about single dads and how they were messing up their kids. This was one
more example of gender inequity in broadcasting . . . But the interviewer interrupted my inner pontificating by raising some of these concerns
herself. I was interested to hear the researcher's response. I listened on.

The answers startled me. The researcher made no judgments or predictions. She rendered no verdicts on women raising children alone.
Rather, she applauded their efforts. She simply said that her findings suggested *kids needed to practice how to behave with members of the opposite
sex.* Long before they dated or went to prom, girls needed to practice
being with boys, and boys needed to practice being with girls. They needed to eat sandwiches together and kick soccer balls together and play in
garage bands together. In short, there were millions of moments when

children had the opportunity to practice how to behave with members of the opposite sex, and a lot—not all, but definitely a whole bunch of that practice—happened in the home. "It does not have to be Dad," the academic emphasized. That role model, that "practice person," could be any adult—an uncle, a grandfather, a close family friend. But the important part was that it needed to be a guy. And he needed to be around all the time.

At that point, I did turn the radio off. I knew this stuff. I had read resilience studies in graduate school about how kids needed someone, anyone, they could count on to navigate those tricky teenage years. Plenty of kids, especially those from tough backgrounds, turned out just fine, and credited the role a teacher or mentor played in their lives. I had prided myself on being that person for some of my students. But I kept coming back to one thought: despite being married, I was a single mom a majority of the time. My girls did not have a practice guy in our home. Because of the choices Ken and I had made these past few years—him pursuing adventures outside of our home and me pursuing purpose within it—we had been depriving our children of their Dad.

Our move to Ohio made sense for a lot of reasons: good health care from Ken's firm, proximity to my family for Lizzie's recoveries, great hospitals all around. But now that Lizzie was through her most difficult operations, were those reasons still valid? Ken and I were well established in this balanced imbalance of ours. He was committed to his work in LA, and I was tethered to my support network in Ohio. But perhaps we had underestimated the effect this agreement might have on our children, especially down the line.

A little absence may warm other people's hearts, but too much can have a chilling effect. Sometimes absence is just absence, emptiness, and loss. With extended periods apart, I had to admit that Ken and I were also growing apart. With the kids, my church involvement, and the care of the house, I did not miss Ken that much. With his all-consuming new job, his commitment to helping veterans find purpose and adventure serving as disaster responders, Ken probably did not have time to miss me much either. But Ken was missing everything with the kids. Something had to change. Or, in our case: someone.

I hate moving. I hate putting stuff in boxes. I hate carrying things up and down stairs. I hate loading stuff onto trucks. And I hate opening boxes in a new state only to discover I could have avoided some schlepping had I only given away more tchotchkes and bric-a-brac. I should be good at it by now. After nearly a decade with Ken in the Navy and nearly a decade with him out, we have relocated together nine times. That does not include all the temporary moves in and out of officer quarters or the times we've moved in with our families while we house-hunted. We've physically transported ourselves and all of our worldly belongings completely across the length of these United States on three separate occasions. Despite my love of impressionism, cubism, and vintage art nouveau, I no longer want to hang pictures on our walls because I so loathe taking them down and boxing them up again. We Harbaughs are like hermit crabs. We try on a shell, and for a while, it feels just right. Then something changes, we grow or yearn or discover, and off we wander to find a new home.

But the Ohio house was different. When we first walked through it with our realtor, I said, "This is the first place I can imagine having grandchildren." In E. M. Forster's *Howards End*, a portion of the plot revolves around Margaret Schlegel and whether she should or should not have been the recipient of a home—Howards End—bequeathed to her by a wealthy, older companion, Mrs. Wilcox. The elder woman's wishes are ignored after her death, and Margaret is initially denied the homestead. But (spoiler alert) after many years, several romances, and a few untimely deaths, Margaret and her belongings end up in Howards End after all, where, it is observed by members of the Wilcox family, those items appear as if they were meant to fit all along. Margaret's belongings belonged in Howards End. That home was a place intended just for them.

That is how I felt in my Chagrin Falls house. As I unboxed painting after painting during our first snowy January, the walls seemed perfectly positioned to receive my artwork. The spot above the fireplace connected effortlessly with the signed painting by the Japanese master. The living room was already decorated with a pale blue that echoed the fog around our Seattle seascape. There was even a nook for the numbered watercolor painting of my hometown—Medina, Ohio—gifted to me years ago by a dear friend. Our life within the house even came to echo the art we hung there. Our dinner parties and barbecues seemed merely an extension of *Luncheon of the Boating Party* hanging in the kitchen. I served formal tea beneath a crystal chandelier we had unearthed in a Charleston thrift shop. My children's toys lay haphazardly beneath the image of a colorful horse from an antique merry-go-round. My belongings seemed like fixtures of the house, and the house seemed a fixture of me. I did not want to break up any of it.

Either Ken had to leave the first job he ever loved or I had to leave my safe harbor.

9 NEVER SAIL INTO A HARBOR YOU CANNOT SAIL OUT OF

One of my favorite windows in that home looked upon a forest of trees that, devoid of their leaves in winter, edged the waterfall and river far below. I sat at that window one night beside a painting of that very same house that Ken had commissioned for our thirteenth wedding anniversary. I sipped a mug of tea and gazed upon the winter wonderland that appeared each and every time the snow fell and outlined those thousands of leafless branches. My dog slept at my feet, and my children were safe in their beds. I had never felt more at home anywhere in my entire life. But was my individual comfort worth the strain it had placed on my marriage? Did I love these four walls more than I loved the father of my children? The answers were right there, but I did not want to utter them aloud. Either Ken had to leave the first job he ever loved or I had to leave my safe harbor.

That became clear to me the day Niagara froze.

12: WHEN LIFE GIVES YOU LEMONADE

That day we spent in Niagara Falls, pacing along the ice-covered catwalk and staring at the frozen falls, I was not thinking about the cold. Sure, it was bone-chilling, toe-curling weather. But we had hats and coats. And we were huddled together in the face of it. I was actually thinking about lemonade.

When the winter weather finally broke, to Lizzie and Katie, that meant one thing: lemonade stands. Our eldest child in particular is a natural entrepreneur, and since she first learned to count, Katie has searched for ways to turn the act of having fun into the art of making money. One winter in Connecticut, she went door to door selling firewood. Our first fall in Ohio, she sold milkshakes and painted rocks. But early spring and summer always brought forth the lemonade stand.

I was on the road so much that I often missed these sales events, usually coming home just in time to deal with the aftermath. So when I pulled into the driveway one night after a week in Los Angeles, I was not surprised to see a sticky folding table blocking the driveway and several soggy Dixie cups scattered on the lawn. Grumbling, I carried the young tycoons' trash to the garage.

I checked the till—about ten bucks in loose change and dollar bills. At twenty-five cents a cup, that seemed a pretty good take for watered-down Country Time. I made a mental note to hose the sidewalk off in the morning and hustled inside to hear the sounds of giggling coming from upstairs. For once, I had not missed bedtime.

That weekend together was good—like most weekends home. Henry and I napped together on the couch. The girls and I caught crawfish in the creek. Annmarie got to yoga—she's always nicer when she gets her *Namaste* on. And I broke out the grill for burgers and bratwurst. But then, it was Sunday night, and I was preparing to leave again.

Before bed, Katie handed me a shoebox.

"What's this?" I asked.

"I've been saving it," she said. She lifted the lid, revealing a pile of change and wads of bills.

"This is great, sweetheart," I said, proud of her for not spending it all at the Popcorn Shop downtown. "What's it for?"

She laid the box in my lap, put her arms around me, and said, "It's for you, Daddy. So you won't have to go away to work tomorrow."

I thought about canceling my meetings for the week, about telling my staff to get by without me. But I was our family breadwinner. And I had my other family to think about—Team Rubicon was in the middle of another disaster response, and I could not simply go AWOL. I talked to Katie about responsibility, about what it meant to provide for loved ones while doing something that mattered. I held her tight, probably a little too long.

After she went to bed, I realized what I should have said.

"Sweetheart, I promise you we will open our own stand together, and we'll sell firewood in the winter and painted rocks in the fall and lemonade all summer long."

But I didn't say that. Instead, I rationalized. I made excuses. After all, we seemed happy, or, at least, content. Annmarie and the kids had Chagrin Falls. I had the best job in the world and had settled into a comfortable rhythm alternating between work weeks in LA and weekends with the family in Ohio.

The truth is, my geo-bachelor life in Southern California was pretty great. When I needed to, I was able to work long hours without worrying about coming home late. When Team Rubicon was running complicated relief operations, I kept a cot in my office and sometimes slept there. *Sans* family, I did everything on my terms. My tiny apartment had all I needed, which was not much. A mattress on the floor, a chair and a table in the kitchen. No TV, no pots or pans, almost nothing in the fridge. More often than not, dinner was a foil pouch of tuna fish with a squeeze of lemon. At home in Ohio, that never would have passed as a meal. But in LA, my weekly shopping trip took less than five minutes: cereal, milk, bananas, tomatoes, lemons, lettuce, and a couple bags of tuna.

Life in California wasn't just easy; it was fun. Every morning, I woke up early and headed to the water. Though I had surfed a bit with Katie, I was still pretty terrible compared to the pros at my local LA break. So I joined the dawn patrol, determined to earn my place in the lineup. The results were mixed. In my first month, I snapped a friend's longboard clean in half trying to ride double overhead waves (beginner tip: bigger waves require smaller boards). During afternoons when the sea breezes picked up, I spent my lunch hour kitesurfing. Like the Chesapeake had been years earlier, the South Bay became my new playground.

One weekend, my flight home was canceled due to snow. "Just stay," Annmarie insisted. "By the time you get here, you'll just have to turn around and go back. Relax. Enjoy yourself." I followed my wife's advice and set out in my station wagon in search of good wind. The forecast indicated steady afternoon breezes a couple hours north along a wide-open section of the coastline named, rather unimaginatively, Surf Beach. Google Earth showed a five-mile stretch of sand near Vandenberg Air Force Base with a single parking lot at the northern tip. By the time I reached my destination, the wind was howling.

The parking lot turned out to be an Amtrak station. Except for a listing porta-potty at one end, the scene was straight out of an old Western—no buildings, no attendant, just an open platform against the rails. There were a few cars in the lot, with a couple people waiting, I assumed, for the next train. The beach, however, was deserted. I lugged my surfboard and kite across the tracks and onto the sand. The wind was blowing hard, driving tiny grains like thousands of needles against my ankles. As the waves pounded the shore, I felt like some hero surfing pioneer discovering a hidden beach.

I launched my kite, hooked into my harness, and headed out. For the next thirty minutes, I battled the surf in search of a path into the open water beyond. My moment came, and darting between two massive sets, I finally reached the rolling waves a half mile offshore. For another hour, I cruised along the coast, completely in my element. All my worldly cares disappeared—work, wife, kids—none of it registered.

Every so often, I glanced back at the parking lot to regain my bearings. A crowd began to form. At first, it was a few people gathered on the platform. Then they migrated to the beach, and every time I looked, there were more. Now I felt like a superstar. When my arms began to give out, I planned my approach back in. A big set rolled past, and as the last wave broke, I followed it, riding the whitewater all the way onto the sand. I popped off my board, scooped it under my arm, and trotted toward the crowd.

A scraggly-looking dude, showing off an impressive surfer tan, greeted me as I approached.

"That was gnarly," he said.

"Yeah," I said, "big waves today." I nodded at the crowd and smiled. "Guess I put on a show."

"Not really, man. We were just waiting to see if you got eaten."

I gave him a funny look.

"Bro, that's Surf Beach," he said. "Only the crazies ride here. This is where we feed guys like you to the great whites."

The moment I got home, I hopped online. The last two fatal shark attacks in California had occurred right there, on that five-mile stretch of coastline. One article referred to the "Great White Serial Killer" of Surf Beach. Another described the deepwater channel running from a drop-off ten miles out. When I took a closer look at Google Earth, there it was, a shark highway directing the great whites straight toward the coastline to prey on seals and sea lions. And, occasionally, the showoff surfer with a hero complex.

My solo adventures were not always that dumb. Another bachelor weekend, I headed south, hitting every surf spot on the map, one crowded with Marines from Camp Pendleton, another overrun by college kids from USC (I preferred the Marines). I kept my station wagon packed with my boards and a wetsuit, and whenever the wind picked up, I launched a kite and let the breeze carry me offshore. One afternoon, as I was riding off Port Hueneme, I found myself in a pod of dolphins. I had ridden with these magnificent animals before, but this group was especially playful. There was a baby in the pod who seemed particularly curious about me. It would dart away from its mother's side, swim alongside my board for a few seconds, then rush back to mama. Normally, the dolphins I encountered were hunting. They surfaced briefly for a breath then disappeared beneath the waves to pursue their prey. But this pod was on a dolphin vacation. They stayed near the surface, swimming laps around me, and every time I popped off a wave for a jump, one of them leapt out of the water nearby. Occasionally, they would spin as they flew through the air. It felt like we were in some kind of interspecies throw-down.

When I got back to the car, I called Annmarie. I had just experienced one of the most thrilling encounters of my life and was desperate to share it with someone. She did not pick up. Often, when she was driving the kids or doing their bedtime routine, she did not have time to talk. That night, I laid awake thinking about my life alone in LA, about the difference between being content and being happy. California felt like endless summer, the kind of harbor I might never sail out of. Yet at the end of every day, however amazing it may have been, there was an ache.

I missed Annmarie. I missed our kids. I missed sharing my adventures with them. And I knew they, too, wanted to share their days with me. I may have found contentment living this way, but I was not *truly* happy.

When Niagara froze, when I stood on that ice-slicked catwalk with my family around me, I thought about what it would take to open a lemonade stand in California. I would have to trade my bachelor life in LA for one that included my kids. No more surfer weekends. No more tuna dinners. They would have to leave their safe Chagrin Falls harbor, Annmarie's family, and all the friends they had come to love. My kids would adjust, but I worried about my wife. Once again, I was asking her to move across the country because I had found my joy and purpose somewhere else. It all seemed horribly unfair. But she saw past the sunshine and palm trees. She knew the great work Team Rubicon was doing and how much it meant to me to be doing it. And, somehow, she reframed her sacrifice as yet another adventure, one the whole family could embark upon together.

The day after Niagara, we called a realtor.

THE SOFA TEST

Annmarie and I have moved many times. When I was in the Navy, I joined a new squadron every three years, sometimes more often. You would think at some point, we would have gotten better at boxes, U-Hauls, and goodbyes. But leaving a place you love is never easy. In the beginning, you think about the lifestyle inconveniences—how nobody's panang curry will ever compare to Thai Awesome's in Hamden, Connecticut, or how you'll never have a drive to work as majestic as Interstate 5 to Interstate 90 in Seattle when Mount Rainier peeks out from the clouds. After that, you become caught up in the details of the move—the truck, the storage, the online forms to shut off the Internet, the water, the heat. Then, as the day creeps closer, you tackle the goodbyes. In the Navy, and even in the nonprofit sector, I knew I would see fellow airmen and team members again. But Annmarie had it much harder. She crumbled leaving every school where she taught and every community that had offered her a home. More recently, both of us had felt the heartache of leaving a place where you have raised your children together. You are leaving their favorite playground, library, and ice cream shop. But more importantly, you are leaving the friends who helped you raise them. The folks who babysat and barbecued and carpooled to soccer or tennis or swimming. The people who told you not to worry about it when your kid burped the entire alphabet or peed on the neighbor's cat. Goodbyes were never easy. And in Chagrin Falls, with Annmarie's parents nearby and with neighbors who had supported her all those years I was away, it was really difficult for my wife to make the decision to leave.

We loved our house, with its crooked staircases and views of the river. We thought we could live there forever. We added to it—nothing major, but the kind of things that portended a future. We redid the masonry around the chimney and put a deep sump pump in the basement to handle rain in the spring. Annmarie planted gardens in the yard that produced enough tomatoes, green beans, broccoli, and zucchini to feed us half the summer. Shadow, our old lab, knew all his favorite spots. He sniffed every corner when we moved in and stood guard at the windows on dark nights.

We even raised chickens. Four brown hens that lived in a coop in the backyard, pecking at bugs and eating whatever kitchen scraps Annmarie threw out the window. They were part of the family, too, and taught the girls better than any book how full of wonder nature can be. Katie and Lizzie raised them from chicks—made sure they had enough grit for their gizzards and fresh water for their bellies. We brought them inside in winter when their water trough iced up, and in summer, the kids took them down the slide on the swing set in the yard.

On Sunday mornings, I got up early, snuck down to the coop, and gathered whatever our hens had laid. It never ceased to be magic that chickens turned insects and vegetable peels into breakfast for our family. When poached, the yolks were the color of sunsets, so orange they seemed almost red. In all the years we had them, the chickens led to only one argument—what to call them? My girls insisted on Mango, Pineapple, Brownie, and Sunshine, but I knew my birds by their real names: Cacciatore, Piccata, Parmigiana, and Cordon Bleu. When their egg-laying years were over, I had always contended we would turn them into the delicious meals after which they were named. We toyed with the idea of bringing the birds with us on the cross-country jaunt. *Why did the chicken cross the road? Because we drove it to California.* But in the end, both sentiment and sense prevailed. We neither ate them nor moved them. Annmarie found our birds a comfortable retirement farm surrounded by goats and ducks and a few older hens just like them.

Everything about our lives in Chagrin said *stay.* Everything, that is, except my absence. As we met with realtors and prepared to abandon this safe harbor, I wondered whether we were making the right choice. Even with all my travel, we had it pretty great there. But whenever I had my doubts about selling the house and uprooting my family, I remembered the lemonade stand. I repeated the promise I had made to myself, that I would be a more present dad. And a better partner in the kids' sidewalk businesses.

We knew leaving Chagrin would take an emotional toll. What we did not anticipate was the amount of stuff we would have to contend with. In the end, moving a house is as much about physics as it is about feelings. Surveying the accumulated clutter of our years of marriage, I nearly seized up. We had so many *things.* A two-hundred-year-old butcher block that we never used, except as an occasional changing table for our kids. An inflatable catamaran that never held air and that we never managed to sail. An upholstered ottoman in the shape of a bear that issued clouds of dust every time we slapped it. We had more toys than we could count, piles of clothes we had never worn, and a whole closet full of tiny shampoos and mouthwashes I had collected from hotels and never used. Where would we even begin?

We started winnowing. Our California house would be tiny, perhaps one-fifth the size of our current residence. We simply could not bring it all. Twenty times a day, we had to decide what was worth carting across the country. What really mattered? It turned out: most things did not. We realized that much of what we owned was weighing us down. The winnowing turned into an awakening. It was occasionally sad to let go of a beloved item—like the gliding chair in which we had fed all three of our babies or the Italian crib where they had all slept. But these things could bring another family joy, and it was liberating to see boxes and bags and a broken boat exiting the house.

The kids got a bit more leeway. Where many of our possessions stifled us, theirs brought them comfort. Katie got to bring her books. Lizzie, her dolls. Henry, his bag of stuffed owls. But to their credit, all three children approached the move with an abiding sense of charity. Every time we went through their closets and drawers, they looked for things to give away.

In the midst of the chaos, my mind flashed back to Annmarie's and my first move together as college kids, leaving our dorm for a cross-country trek that turned into . . . well, *this*. Nineteen years earlier, we had packed nearly everything we owned, Tetris-style, into the back of my beat-up grey Pathfinder. For all Annmarie's insistence that we were just having fun, that we would *never get married*, that trip turned into a life together.

If you ever want to know whether you are with the right person, if you have chosen the right life partner, move furniture together. Annmarie and I carried a couch to the front entryway only to become stuck and realize that it needed to go back upstairs and down the other staircase to exit via the garage door. If I still had my chainsaw, I would have cut that thing in half. Instead, we hauled it back up and down the stairs. Yes, indeed—if you can move a sofa together, you can get married and stay married. If you can laugh when the kitchen table doesn't fit through the door, if you can apologize when you skin her knuckles

Annmarie and I carried a couch to the front entryway only to become stuck and realize that it needed to go back upstairs. If I still had my chainsaw, I would have cut that thing in half.

| I | ADVENTURES ARE WORTH THE MISHAPS |

on the banister, if she can forgive you when you scratch the hardwood floor, you can navigate a lifetime.

When the packing was finished, we had fit everything we owned into the back of a twelve-foot Ryder truck. We tried to do everything one last time. One more trip to the Popcorn Shop, one more hike to the river. I said goodbye to the house. Our family had made so many memories there, mostly good ones. I paused a moment at the azalea in the front yard, the one we'd planted after the miscarriage. As I bid farewell, even the sad memories felt worth holding onto.

I climbed into the truck and set off for a solo cannonball run across the United States. We had wanted to drive together, but since we were moving ourselves, that meant we would either have to travel 2,600 miles in separate vehicles or someone would need to make two trips. Annmarie stayed behind to pack up the kids and the dog, do a final once-over, and hand the keys to the new owners. My plan was to get to LA, move into the new house, and have everything ready to welcome the family. Then I would fly back to Ohio to repeat the trek with Annmarie and the kids.

With the truck's speed regulator pegged out at sixty-five miles per hour, and with a few catnaps in truck-stop parking lots, I made the trip in two and a half days. Despite my fatigue and the fast food wrappers piling up on the passenger seat, the scenery outside amazed me: the seemingly endless Great Plains halted only by etchings of mountains far in the distance; the deer signs that had me on my toes at dusk; the dust devils in the desert; the cacti spotting the hillsides; the trains that stretched for miles; and, most of all, the road.

As I pulled into the driveway of our new home, I was met by a posse of Team Rubicon greyshirts. I had asked one to help me unload the truck. Ten showed up. It had taken Annmarie and me three days to load up, but within thirty minutes, the back was empty and we were moved in. Looking around the new house, it occurred to me that the entire floor plan—two tiny bedrooms, a living room, and a galley kitchen—would have fit inside our living room back in Ohio. In spite of the tiny space, it felt right.

The following weekend, I was on a plane headed back to Ohio to repeat the trip with the family. As I settled into my seat, I received an email from Annmarie. Those final days in Chagrin had been a whirlwind. She had been positively overwhelmed by the outpouring of help, cleaning supplies, and love. The email read:

From : Annmarie Kelly-Harbaugh

Date: June 18, 2014 at 9:52:06 PM

Subject: One last goodbye

It did indeed take a village . . .

But the van is finally packed and we are well on our way.

Huge thank-yous to everyone who took pity on my discombobulation and mayhem and stopped by the house over the past few weeks.

This includes, but is not limited to:

The friend who stuffed her minivan full of my trash and recycling.

The friend who swept up four years of dog hair using a plastic broom and a placemat.

The friend who packed my pantry fiasco into three tidy boxes.

The friend who took my kids away so I could rage at my inability to pack anything in a timely fashion.

The friend who brought pizza.

The friend who brought boxes.

The friend who brought salad and chocolate.

The friend who stayed by my side for the final, teary-eyed walkthrough of our empty house.

The friend who walked us to the Popcorn Shop one last time.

The friends who invited my kids on playdates, who sang show tunes, and who carted the kids to Dazzle, the duck pond, the playground, and the pool.

The friend who worked out with me for the last time and dragged me through fifty-six burpees and weighted squats.

And if I failed to list you above, or if I failed to say one last in-person goodbye, it is only because I am exhausted and still grieving at the thought of leaving all of you wonderful folks behind. As I have said before, if I had a little gumption and a slightly larger sack, I would take you with me.

The good news is we'll be back. In late September. And plenty of Christmases and summer vacations after that.

In the meantime, there are plenty of ways to find us. Via email, Facebook, or Instagram. Or at our new place in California.

And whether I hear from you weekly from now until forever or we simply fade into the background like old friends are prone to do, please know that you Chagrin guys and gals will always hold a special place in my heart. Thanks for having my back. Whether mountains divide us or time zones or years, please know that I will always have yours.

I love you all,

Annmarie

Happiness is cheap—we discovered that truth once again. Leaving Chagrin, we realized what was most important, what made a life: people, relationships, the memories you make and share with others. I was convinced that at our new home, we would make more, and we would make them together.

CROSS COUNTRY—TAKE TWO

When I landed in Ohio, it felt like a very different place. The Harbaughs no longer lived there. I did not drop by the old house or drive through the old town. Annmarie picked me up at the airport with our van packed to the gills, and after a few days with her parents, we hit the road. The trip felt comfortably reminiscent of that first cross-country trek with Annmarie back in college. This time, instead of a beat-up Pathfinder, we had the proverbial family minivan, brimming with kids, clothes, and anticipation. We visited friends along the way and dropped in on a reunion for my mom's side of the family at a New Orleans bowling alley. They had hired a photographer, and we sat for our first family portrait. In it, we look nonsensical. My mother had given the girls matching dresses for the picture. One was too big, the other too small, but they donned them anyway to be polite. Katie is putting a bow in her hair. Lizzie has slapped her nametag across her face. Annmarie is holding Henry by the scruff of his T-shirt because he is trying to run away. I am laughing at the whole fiasco. Of the five of us, only Annmarie is looking at the camera and smiling wryly. We still have that photo, and whenever I see it, I smile, too. There we are, a

Leaving Chagrin, we realized what was most important, what made a life: people, relationships, the memories you make and share with others.

3 · HAPPINESS IS CHEAP

family at sea, completely disheveled but together and happy. Although we had left our safe harbor and still had plenty of questions about where we were headed, we did not feel at all lost.

A week later, we arrived in Los Angeles. As we approached the driveway, I told Annmarie to keep going. Our house was at the top of a hill, beyond which lay the sand dunes and the ocean. We had been on the road all day, and the sun was approaching the horizon.

"Just a little farther," I said.

"Are you crazy?" she said. "We've been driving for thirty-five hours. We're done."

"Trust me," I pleaded. "Five more minutes—it's why we came."

"Fine," she said. We crested the hill and saw the Pacific stretched out before us. To the north were the Santa Monica Mountains. To the south, the cliffs of Palos Verdes, with the windows of a hundred villas reflecting the setting sun.

The kids' eyes went wide.

"Is that the ocean?" Lizzie asked.

"Yep," I said. "And it goes all the way to Japan."

"Can we go in?" Katie asked.

Annmarie glanced over at me. I could read her mind. She and the kids had been living out of that van for nearly two weeks—visiting, driving, eating trashy food, driving more. She had not had a break. Annmarie wanted to tap out. Go for a run. Get a shower. Decompress. The last thing she wanted at that very moment was to take the kids to the beach. But my wife is an expert at situational awareness. She knew they were anxious about the move, about living in California. Annmarie knew we had to make the long journey feel worth it. Every adventure had its destination. We were finally looking at ours. She glanced at Katie, smiled, and said, "Let's go for a swim."

Day one in California saw the Harbaughs, fully clothed, running into the ocean from a minivan bursting at the seams with pillows, suitcases, and dreams of a new life together. Henry rolled in the sand. Lizzie looked for crabs and danced in the surf. And Katie, Annmarie, and I jumped up and down in the waves.

We got back to the house just before dark, soaking wet and covered in sand. All three kids ran through the place exploring, imagining bunk beds and forts and a thousand ways to turn this tiny home into a castle. Before we could corral them into the tub, they discovered the backyard. Standing on tippy toes, we gazed over the fence at the shimmering sea. As the little ones stared in wonder, Katie's eyes drifted to the solitary tree in the far corner of the yard. It was in shadows, and the outline was hard to make out. Katie squinted at it and then looked at me.

"Dad, is that a *lemon* tree?" she asked.

"Yep," I said. "And the lemons are ready to be picked."

That first summer in California was everything I hoped. We caught waves; we rode bikes; we ate fish tacos. Even Shadow, our old black lab, found a new lease on life. Once again, he investigated every corner of the new house and deemed it safe for us to inhabit. This one had no stairs for him to negotiate, just a straight shot out the kitchen door to the big backyard. The weather suited him, and he found a new favorite spot in the shade of a certain tree.

We have less of almost everything now. Less space, less money, less stuff. But we do have each other and a lemon tree in our backyard. And since this is California, where it is always summer, our lemonade stand stays busy all year long.

13: CHASING DRAGONS

Los Angeles is a funny place to live. On the one hand, it is beautiful. It is 70 degrees and sunny most of the year, and a good portion of LA County abuts the Pacific Ocean. But Los Angeles is also gross. Nine million people live here. There is pollution, crime, traffic, and sprawl. From our two-bedroom house in El Segundo, we can stroll to the ocean, but we can also walk to the freeway, an oil refinery, a sewage treatment plant, and Los Angeles International Airport. We are less than a day's drive away from some of the country's greatest natural wonders—Yosemite, the Grand Canyon, the Mojave desert—but the sheer number of people trying to navigate this city all but guarantees that such destinations are at least one headache and many hours of traffic away. Unless your journeys have a purpose, Los Angeles can make you feel like staying home. But with our family together more often now, weekends often find us braving the mayhem in pursuit of new adventures.

One of our recent jaunts found us in Pacifica, an out-of-the-way surfing town just south of San Francisco. The surroundings were enchanting, but our hotel room was stuffy and uncomfortable, so after a shabby night's sleep, I headed out for a morning hike. I meandered along a trail high above the ocean, and it was glorious—blue-green water, salty air, sweeping vistas. I breathed deep and felt lucky. Here we were. In California. Together. We had neither wealth nor fame nor power, but we had love, purpose, and good kids.

It was warmer than I had anticipated, so before heading up the switchback, I zipped down to the car for sunscreen and a hat. In the hotel parking lot, I hesitated. This day was too amazing to keep all to myself. I ventured upstairs to grab the family.

Our three precious yahoos were sitting in the in-room bathtub eating mini muffins, drinking apple cider, and watching the Disney Channel. Ken was asleep.

"I found an awesome trail!" I chirped. "Who's up for a hike?"

No one answered.

"Hey, guys. Anyone want to come hiking?"

Still nothing. I stepped in front of the television.

"Mom, I can't see the TV." "Move." "Ugh!"

Ken muttered that he would like to come, but then he rolled over and went back to sleep.

That should have been my cue. They were on vacation. They had muffins. And crappy TV. They were happy. Not everything in a family needs to be shared.

But we had worked so hard to make moments like this possible. I muted the program to clarify my vision—the blue-green water, that crisp sea air. Again, there were protests. Katie reminded me that children do not care about such things. I could have headed for the hills alone. Instead, I cajoled, complained, and insisted. Had we driven six hours to watch television? Didn't family time always make us happy?

After you live with folks for a while, you learn their particular kind of crazy. When Ken and the kids realized I was not going to let this drop, they begrudgingly acquiesced. It took nearly ninety minutes, but eventually, everyone was dried, dressed, and sunscreened for the transcendent family outing I had declared. We set off up the hill.

It was strange to be ascending with people so obviously downtrodden.

It was hotter now than when I had originally set out. My formerly energetic pace was quickly slackened by grumbles, quarrels, and literal foot-dragging.

"I'm hot."

"Walking is dumb."

"I can't believe we're missing *A.N.T. Farm* for this."

I should have left them at the hotel. What kind of idiot drags kids out of a bathtub to hike? If and when we ever finished this dirty ramble, they were just going to need another bath. I had desperately wanted to share this sojourn with them, and as soon as we began sharing it, I desperately wanted them to go away.

The kids made me cranky and I made them crankier, and various threats were lobbed regarding the abandonment of the entire business, but we kept trudging forward anyway—me because I refused to return to the hotel yet again without first climbing this blasted hill, and them because . . . well, they are kids, and kids are prone to follow trails and sidewalks until they end. Shel Silverstein taught us that.

What began as a swift, splendid hike by myself turned into a slow, terrible hike with the children. But here's the thing—it's actually really hard to stay angry at your kids when:

A. You are exercising.

B. You see beauty.

C. You realize your kids have stopped being angry at you.

For about eleven minutes, our slog became kind of awesome. We reached the summit. We caught a lizard. We followed a secret trail and ate wild fennel. We even made it halfway back to the car before everyone fell apart again. Someone had rocks in her shoe. Someone else was angry about his hat.

That's the funny thing about doing anything with children. It does not matter where we go—a restaurant, a water park, the bathroom—taking them with us makes the excursion more difficult. It is tempting to avoid outings altogether. That hike was different because our kids were there. It was so much worse but also a little better. I have stood on a mountaintop before. But they never had. I have hiked through blisters and sunburns, discomfort and thirst, and have been rewarded by majesty at the trail's end. But they never had. I have never summited Everest. At the rate my pants are not fitting, it may not ever be in the cards. But I imagine that the only thing greater than climbing a tremendous peak is enabling someone else to climb it with you. The only thing better than a sunset is a sunset that you share. On such journeys, adventure and purpose meet.

It can be exhausting to teach our kids adventure, but it is more frustrating still to teach them complacency. I want our kids to comfort the broken, defend the weak, and minister to those in need. These are not always natural acts. They require confidence and bravery. And I dare say they begin with simple steps, even rocky, bedraggled, complaint-riddled steps on a hill overlooking the Pacific.

Camping Alone. With Kids.

We went camping a few months ago. No place fancy, just some car pull-in at a state campground north of the city. Ken and I have been toying with the idea of a larger trip—maybe to Sequoia National Park or Joshua Tree—and we wanted to see first how the kids did on a scaled-back version.

The kids did fine. Children are natural campers. They were excited about the tent, the sleeping bags, the lanterns, the Swiss army knife, and the nesting pots and pans. The only thing that disappointed them was me.

"That's not the way Dad does it," Katie pointed out as I arranged tinder for the fire. "Have you ever even lit a campfire before, Mom?"

"I camped for a living for two years before you were born," I replied.

"Liar," she said. It occurred to me that my children have no sense of the person I was before I had them. I was independent, tenacious, and chock full of wilderness skills—before they came along and peed on everything.

They looked positively amazed when I boiled a pot of noodles over the open fire. Together, we cooked macaroni and cheese and hot dogs, cocoa and s'mores. And that night in the tent, with our kids asleep all around us, I turned to Ken and said, "We should do this more often."

And even though everyone cried at breakfast—over clean-up, a skinned knee, and the absence of Cheerios—I still meant it. Camping is the family equivalent of a cheap date. Throw a blanket and some ramen noodles in the back of the car, and you are all set.

That's why, in February, I took the kids camping alone.

Ken was overseas for business. Katie was visiting Auntie Ruth and Uncle Kito. Which left the little ones and I in need of entertainment. Lizzie, in particular, is a camping aficionado, and so I told her we would sleep outside and toast some marshmallows. To be fair, I had meant in our backyard. I had no intention of schlepping two young children hours into the Los Angeles forest for some creepy campout. I'm pretty sure they film horror movies up there. So I tried to convince Lizzie and Henry to camp in the yard. But Lizzie would not be deterred. She wanted an adventure to "somewhere we've never been, Mom."

Begrudgingly, I researched campsites that seemed both safe and magical and found one nestled in a canyon, with trees for shade, other campers for company, and trails down to the ocean. Since it was Valentine's Day weekend, I checked availability online. They would not take reservations less than twenty-four hours in advance, but the schedule said they had walk-up sites available. That was good enough for me. Together, my six-year-old, my three-year-old, and I packed for our trip.

Lizzie thought of nearly everything: blankets, pillows, sleeping bags, noodles, peanut butter sandwiches, graham crackers, marshmallows, chocolate, and baby wipes. Henry grabbed two armfuls of stuffed animals. I grabbed the tent and filled some water jugs, and we were off. To the wild green yonder. To prove that camping alone with Mom could be awesome, too.

The night before, Google Maps predicted we could travel the thirty-seven miles to our campsite in seventy-one minutes. That afternoon, however, as is often the case in Los Angeles, home to the worst traffic I have ever experienced, we covered that distance in just under three hours. We stopped briefly for gas, Cheetos, and firewood and then puttered up the coast, braking 752 more times behind every cheapskate Angelino in Christendom who also seemed to be camping on Valentine's Day.

When we finally arrived at our safe but magical campsite, we were greeted by a stern-faced woman who would have immediately become my least favorite aunt had she been a member of my family. *No, of course, the campground had no room. No, she could not explain why the website had indicated there was space available. No, she could not possibly find a patch of dirt anywhere on the thirteen-thousand-acre grounds for us to pitch a tent. No, she could not recommend anywhere else to go. No, I could not park my car in the shade of that tree to figure out our next move.* Each NO was a dart to my heart, and to Lizzie's. How was I supposed to prove that "Mom is awesome at camping" if I could not even accomplish the part of the plan where we, you know, camped?

Because I did not have enough nerve or a heavy enough rock to throw at the lady, the kids and I drove on. I had initially rejected a campsite further up the coast when I read that it frequently had "dangerous winds," but the day was seventy-five degrees and balmy, so I figured we could give it a shot.

Our naysayer at this campground was at least apologetic. He handed me a list of other venues to try and even permitted us to pull off near the ranger booth to make some phone calls. For future reference, a quarter past four on a Sunday afternoon of a holiday weekend turns out to be an inopportune time for firming up camping reservations. I made fourteen phone calls, left eight messages, and spoke to only one human. Sally was the group reservations specialist at a KOA on the other side of the mountains. They were an hour and a half northeast, and fully booked, but she said they'd make room for us if we could make the drive. I was jazzed. We had kindness and a campsite. We were in business.

When I informed the little ones that we needed to get back on the road, there was rebellion. Henry wanted French fries. Lizzie wanted retribution. Not ten feet from where we were parked, she saw people camping. There were dozens of picture-perfect setups, each with an individual fire pit, all overlooking the Pacific Ocean. "Mom, why can't we just stay here?" She was right. This was nonsense. After the traffic we had endured just to get here, there was no telling how long the journey would be to the KOA. Sunset was around five thirty. Even if we did make it, we would be pitching our tent in darkness. There was plenty of room right here.

"Let's go ask the nice man again," I said.

Sometimes adults will bring small children with them to request something they know would be denied if they simply asked alone. It is a trifle shameless, but I have employed this strategy at Panera when I want another hunk of sourdough bread. The folks at the register will tell me I have to pay ninety-nine cents for it, but the salad and sandwich artisans in back will usually just give the same bread to my son for free. It is a manipulative maneuver, for sure. But that afternoon, with my camping credentials on the line and sunset imminent, I wielded my kids as weapons. "Excuse me, sir," I said to the park ranger, who looked more like a bored fifteen-year-old than a person in a position of outdoor authority. "Are you sure you don't have anywhere we could pitch our little tent?"

"I'm sorry, you guys," he said to the kids. Again, he seemed genuinely apologetic. "All the campsites are rented out tonight."

"What if we waited a little bit? Do you ever have cancellations?" I asked.

"No, not really," he said. I looked around. Most of the campsites were occupied by Airstreams and Winnebagos, but the beach was wide open.

"What if we put up a tent on the beach?" I asked.

"Each of the campsites includes a section of beach. You would have to be part of an existing group," he explained.

"So all we really need is an invitation to camp with someone already here?" I asked.

He looked at me like I was crazy. "I guess so," he said. "You would just need to come back here and tell me which campsite, so I could give you a reserved parking space. Otherwise, the overnight guy issues tickets."

Which is how Lizzie, Henry, and I ended up walking barefoot up the beach asking total strangers if we could crash with them on Valentine's Day.

Fun fact: most people camping on February 14th are looking for a romantic getaway. Friendly as they may be, they do not wish to share their enchanted campsite with a family of three. We walked through twenty-two sites, past dreamy-eyed couples and rowdy college kids, until we found the Gonzalez family who, with no questions or suspicion or irritation, immediately agreed to let us pitch a tent on their RV site. Jennifer, two sites down, offered us her extra parking space. And Joanna, in the motor home in between, noticed us unloading our car in the fading light and gifted us an inflatable solar flashlight that quickly became my new favorite camping gizmo. After more than an hour being rebuffed by people in charge, in less than ten minutes, the kids and I were welcomed by total strangers. With the sun sinking toward the horizon, we began setting up camp.

Lizzie and I did our best, but it turned out that neither of us had ever put up the new tent before. I was used to our old A-frame, but Ken had upgraded to this four-person jobbie after an end-of-season sale at REI. I understood the

After more than an hour being rebuffed by people in charge, in less than ten minutes, the kids and I were welcomed by total strangers.

5   Talk to Strangers

basic concept, but our poles kept collapsing and the tent stakes would not stick in the sand. Lighting the lantern gave me trouble, too. After twenty years of domesticity, had I lost my camping swagger?

What I lacked in ability, I like to think I made up for in good humor. Plus, our new friends, the Gonzalezes, helped us along. Instead of the tiny roasting sticks Lizzie and Henry had gathered in our driveway, Tom loaned us his hot dog rack, and except for the two and a half wieners I dropped in the fire, we did all right there. His sister, Christina, helped us assemble the tent. And Graciela, the matriarch of the family, shared folding chairs with us as she cuddled her grandbaby near the fire. Lizzie had insisted we bring a box of macaroni and cheese, and Tom's fiancée, Danielle, was kind enough to bring our tiny pot of water to boil on the stove inside their trailer. Lizzie, Henry, and Graciela's other grandchild, Gabriel, ate warm noodles out of red plastic cups and nibbled charred hot dogs with ketchup Gabriel shared from the fridge. They gave us glow sticks, candy hearts, and seats by their fire. We gave them marshmallows, macaroni, and a couple of muffins we had brought for breakfast.

The winds kicked up and the air grew cooler, so just before eight o'clock, Lizzie, Henry, and I brushed our teeth, said goodnight, and turned in. As soon as I unzipped our tent, I was alarmed by how noisy it was. The balmy sea breezes had been replaced by veritable squalls. Our fly tarp flapped against the tent fabric and made a constant *rip-rip-rip* sound. The kids were afraid. I regaled them with stories of their Dad's and my camping trips before they were born. How we canoed to a barrier island in Florida and watched a Space Shuttle launch. How we camped along a rail line in Oregon and how Hound and Shadow barked furiously at each train passing in the darkness. How we rented a boat near Panama City and how, after we failed to anchor it properly, the vessel floated away while we slept.

The kids drowsed as they listened to the flapping of the tent and the cadence of my stories. But they were jarred awake every few minutes when heavy gusts of wind buckled our tent poles and the tent, which was designed to keep out *rain*, let the sand pour right in the top vents onto our faces and hair. I am a pretty good sport. I have slept in temperatures below zero and woken to my boot liners frozen to the floor. I have camped in weather so hot and humid that I chose to be eaten by mosquitos rather than broil inside my sleeping bag. And I once slept on the floor of a men's restroom when my campsite flooded during an autumn downpour. But this sandstorm was something new. It clouded our lungs and settled in the corners of our eyes. And when the gusts pressed the sides of the tent down against our faces, for just a few seconds, none of us could breathe. We squished together in the center of the tent. Eventually, exhausted, the kids fell asleep. I held a blanket above their faces to shield them from the flying sand. I wanted to sleep, too, but there was no way to doze off while holding that blanket umbrella. I dropped it, and sand cascaded once again into my face. I was miserable. All I could think about was my comfortable, clean, and quiet bed thirty-seven miles away. I wanted to go home. But how could I get us out of there without disappointing my kids?

Lucky for me, neither Henry nor Lizzie has any real sense of time. They cannot read clocks, they don't keep track of minutes, and they get spatially loopy around bedtime. So at 8:47 p.m., after what felt like my hundredth drink of sand, I nudged the kids awake and told them we were leaving.

"Why?" asked Lizzie.

"We are heading out super early to get home while there is no traffic," I replied. While this was not technically untrue, I still felt a little guilty saying it. "You can sleep more in the car." Too tired to protest, Lizzie let me carry her to the minivan. Not only did the Gonzalezes not make fun of me when I abandoned ship, they good-humoredly helped me break camp amid the squalls. On the edge of the Pacific Ocean, in the wind advisory that turned out to be real, Christina, Danielle, Tom, and I collapsed that flapping tent beneath thousands of stars. We wished each other a Happy Valentine's Day, and the kids and I drove away.

All in all, we camped for about four hours. We spent more time packing and driving than we did roughing it. I did not impress anyone with my wilderness skills. But Henry and Lizzie got sleeping bags, marshmallows, and hot dogs and the chance to pee twice in a porta-potty chained to the beach. I did not teach either of them how to put up a tent or light a fire, but they learned a skill equally important. When the world tells you "No," seek out the "Yes." Talk to strangers, and do not fear the adventures. Even the sandiest escapades are worth the mishaps.

For days after we returned, when I told friends about our "camping" trip, the comment I heard again and again was, "I can't believe you took them all by yourself." As though we had been climbing Kilimanjaro or harvesting winter wheat. It had been my goal to demonstrate to my children that a woman—even a mom—could survive against the elements. We did not, but I have no doubt that we could next time. Though maybe we'll start with different elements.

In the meantime, the kids learned a lesson in kindness. It is everywhere. Sometimes you just have to look for it. Behind a gruff gatekeeper, past a disinterested teen, kindness is there, flapping in the wind and in the hearts of strangers who will open their motorhome for no other reason than it is the decent thing to do.

Even the sandiest escapades are worth the mishaps.

I ADVENTURES ARE WORTH THE MISHAPS

The Shadow in My Heart

Of course, not all of our exploits in California have led us up rocky precipices or along sandy shores. One of our most difficult journeys took place at home. Shadow, our sixteen-year-old dog, enjoyed a renewed spirit when we moved out here. Rehabilitated by the sea air and sunshine, he surveyed his new backyard and took to napping beneath the lemon tree.

At night, he implemented a rotating shift, sleeping near the kids' beds then finally settling down next to ours.

But after a few months, his rituals began to alter. He took to waking us at four o'clock in the morning, pacing our bedroom, collar jangling, looking for God knows what. He would wander into corners and let out a hoarse *woof.* "He's talking to ghosts," Ken would mutter sleepily, and one of us would stumble out of bed to let him out and feed him a meal we called "first breakfast." Hours later, Shadow would have no memory of the episode, and the whole sad process would repeat itself again.

Before the kids, Shadow and Hound (who died a few years earlier) were our babies. We vacationed with them, road-tripping from one dog-friendly establishment to the next—except for one motel in Iowa where we got totally busted for sneaking them in the back entrance. We exercised together, swam at the beach, and took daytime naps back when that sort of thing was even possible. For many years, they were very, very good to us. Dogs love us the way we wish we could love others. Their hearts are always open. They always understand. They are generosity and forgiveness on four legs.

Which is why it was so difficult when Shadow stopped eating. At first, I thought he had a tummy ache. But after the third day of his hunger strike, I knew. I called Ken at work. Shadow could no longer get up to go outside, and I worried he would pass before Ken got home. But Shadow was too polite for that. When Ken arrived, Shadow was still breathing, but barely. He was lying in his favorite indoor spot, a fur-covered divot in the carpet by Ken's side of the bed. We stretched out on either side of our dog. Slowly and with great effort, he lifted his head and laid it on Ken's arm. Shadow opened an eye and let out a sigh. He was telling us he was done.

Shadow had traveled across the country, settled us into this new home, and made sure we would all be okay here. He had checked every corner and stood watch every night. He had tended to us for sixteen years and had never asked for anything in return—until today. He was tired, and in pain, and he was asking us to take him on his last walk.

When he sighed again, there was something of an apology in it. *I wish I could do this for you*, he seemed to say. Ken pulled the phone from his pocket. The veterinarian said we could come anytime. I left to pick up the kids from school.

I had spent the past few days preparing them. On the drive home, they learned it was time to say goodbye. The kids filtered in, crowding gently around Shadow, running their hands through his fur. Lizzie laid a handful of flowers by his nose, and we told them stories about happier days.

Ken and I adopted Shadow when we lived in Washington State, and he scampered with us all over this nation. He swam in both the Atlantic and the Pacific Oceans and chased tennis balls everywhere from Miami to Seattle. He traveled in sailboats and rowboats and lounged in paddling pools and mud puddles. He was a snuggly little dreamer, a pacifist afraid of fireworks and marching bands, with a little bark and very little bite. Defying our attempts to feed him only dog food, Shadow ate every toaster waffle Henry ever held and unpacked every lunch box Katie or Lizzie ever left on the living room floor, acquiring a taste for tomatoes, cucumbers, and string cheese. And despite his cartoonish affability, he had a penchant for mischief, like the time he followed Lizzie to school or galloped through a wedding ceremony on the beach.

When Ken saw that we were all smiling and thinking about Shadow, he knew it was time to go. We each gave our big black dog one last squeeze, and Ken cradled him in his arms to the car.

Ken took Shadow alone. Lizzie, Katie and I wept together on the couch while Henry jumped on the ottoman and asked for cereal. In my grief, I compared Shadow to a bad boyfriend. "I gave him my love, and he was destined to break my heart," I sobbed. Something about this melodrama was too much for the girls. They laughed, lovingly, at my ridiculous statement. Shadow had no malice in him.

That day was the first time I wept openly with my children. I could not have held it together if I tried. The girls honored my grief and climbed bravely through the difficulties of that afternoon, stepping gingerly around their father's heartache and mine. They understood that—just like Pixar's *Inside Out* taught us—sometimes joy and sadness can both be part of the same hopelessly beautiful moment.

At the animal hospital, Ken asked the vet if he could share one last story before they got started. Dr. Streiber sat on the floor next to them and listened. Ken started to tell about Afghanistan and how it had been this dog that helped settle him back home. Shadow's breathing grew even shallower, and Ken trailed off mid-story. The doc put a reassuring hand on his. "And now this dog is the one in pain," he said. "It is time to lay him to rest."

When Ken came home alone, the kids and I gathered around him on the couch and we talked about heaven. We told them we would see Shadow there, but, of course, in our hearts, we could not be sure.

Four o'clock the next morning, I again awoke to noises, but this time, it was Ken stumbling around in the darkness. Shadow had visited him in a dream. "I saw him across a wide river," he said. "He was wagging his tail and running again." Ken wondered if Shadow was trying to cross back over to him. Then Ken saw his fur, wet from a good swim. Shadow wasn't coming back. He was waiting.

We know now that if there is a heaven, our dogs are the ones who let us in.

Monsters Below

In the months since Shadow's death, we have tried to distract ourselves with the kinds of adventures that were difficult to coordinate when he was alive. We traveled to a wild horse preserve in a canyon on the edge of the Mojave Desert. We pulled the kids out of school to visit Grandma and Grandpa Harbaugh on their farm in San Antonio, and we spent another weekend with Auntie Jenny and Uncle Scott snorkeling with endangered fish in Catalina. But other adventures have occurred closer to home.

The weather has been unseasonably warm here in Southern

California. The mild water temperatures have lured sea creatures to feed closer to shore. Dolphins, sea lions, and seals have all been spotted in greater numbers. Not long ago, it was even rumored there were whales in the bay.

Ken and I decided to see if it was true.

We brought the children with us.

That might have been a mistake.

Like most of our excursions, 66 percent of our kids professed disdain for and disinterest in the initial plan. Lizzie said she would only come if she could bring her new sketchpad. And markers. And applesauce. And a blanket. When we explained that we would be kayaking, she called us "No fun" and hid in her room. When we told Katie our idea, she suggested going for fish tacos instead. When we said we would really like to stick with the whale scheme, and that maybe we could grab food after, she told us we were *ruining her life* and flopped down on the living room floor. Only little Henry agreed to come whale watching with us. He grabbed his five favorite stuffed animals and hopped in the car. It was only later that we learned he had thought we were going to watch whales in a movie theater.

We very nearly left them all at home. Hiring a sitter would have been easier. We were offering them a once-in-a-lifetime maritime excursion, and they were bellyaching as though we had said, "Take out the trash." Despite our best intentions to raise our children with purpose and adventure, not all expeditions begin with enthusiasm. Many . . . most . . . begin with bedlam. It took us nearly two hours of arguments, anger, and bribery, but in the end, we kicked all three children into the car, out of the car, and onto those boats.

To be fair, the kids may have been resistant based on family history. This was not our first endeavor to see majestic ocean life. Last summer, Ken took the kids on a dolphin boat that failed to spot any dolphins and a lobster dive that resulted in zero crustaceans, borderline hypothermia, and a below-average dinner at a Chinese restaurant. So, when it came to the whole whale float plan, maybe the kids were right to be hesitant. But for Ken and me, this day felt different. The leviathans were out there. We just had to find them.

When we procured our two kayaks, the rental gal circled a patch of blue water on a waterlogged tourist map. "Somewhere in there," she said, and assured us that it was only a "quick two- to three-mile paddle" out to where the animals had last been sighted. After a brief conference during which Ken and I ascertained that we had never paddled even half that far with the kids in tow, we threw caution to the wind and shoved off.

The receptionist had described the water as "glassy" when we called to reserve the boats, but by the time we had all of the arguments we need-ed to have—about markers, life-ruining, movies, and tacos—the sea was beginning to churn. Visibility had begun to diminish, waves were march-ing in, and the wind blew steadily onshore.

We paddled in circles in the marina and nearly crashed into the sea wall before we established any semblance of a sculling rhythm. Our pad-dles were identical, but Katie and I argued over them anyway, and Lizzie yelled at Dad because the sea lion colony—which I had found charming and hilarious—was "too smelly to smell." We followed the green cans past the breakwater and out toward open ocean. As we left the shelter of the harbor, we found ourselves looking at fifteen-mile-an-hour winds and three-foot swells. For true sea kayakers, these were probably ideal conditions. But for folks like us, who had eaten hushpuppies for break-fast, it was backbreaking. After the eleventh wave broke over the bow of his boat, Ken suggested we turn back. Considering the rough seas, our laborious progress, and the kids' attitudes, reason was on his side. The children had probably been right about this "dumb stupid trip to see dumb stupid fish."

But sometimes, the more stubborn my kids get, the more obstinate I become. I wasn't ready to fold. "Let's keep going," I said. At least we would get a workout in.

And work out we did.

We pointed our banana-yellow kayaks toward a leaning sailboat along on the horizon and paddled for a solid fifteen minutes as though we might be able to catch it. The water felt so heavy against our paddles, and the current so stiff against our boats, that I was not convinced we were getting anywhere. I was about to turn around when Ken saw the vertical waterspout.

"*Scheisse!*" he screamed. My husband rarely swears, and on the few occasions when he falters, it often comes out in German. He grinned wide-eyed and pointed to a swirling patch of water two hundred yards away. The rest of us had missed it, but we paddled furiously toward the dark water and the promise of a sea creature below.

We had sculled for less than a minute before Katie saw the tail. She pointed and shrieked, "I see it! I see it!" There were squeals from Ken's boat as he and the little ones cut in front of us and paddled toward the spray. Soon, they were pointing and screaming. I still didn't see anything.

Katie and I lagged behind. Our boat was heavier, and she was too excited to help paddle. She turned around to face me. "Mom, did you see that? It was amazing!"

I am the only one in our family who wears glasses. I struggle to see things that are far away. My dollar-store sunglasses merely compound this nearsightedness. Thus I did not see the first whale breach. I did not see the other one slap its tail or poke a nose above the surface. I did not see the water blowing vertically twenty feet into the air. I always seemed to be facing the wrong direction or looking left when the animals had already swum right. All I saw at that moment were the marching waves as I heard Ken yell that the whales were swimming away. I squinted my eyes against the sun glare, scanned the horizon, and pulled up my paddle. Our boat bobbed in the now-empty sea.

I consoled myself. Wasn't it more important that the children saw them? After all, isn't that a mom's job? To be a vehicle of strength and opportunity, to boost kids right up to the wonderful moments, even if that meant never actually witnessing those wonders myself? Even though they had begun the adventure as Jerkasauruses, I knew the kids were going to remember this day for the rest of their lives. The day their mom and dad paddled them into the ocean to see hunormous whales breaching in the bay. I would not ruin the memory by pouting about how I had missed it.

Then, without warning, an enormous dark-grey tail stood straight up in the water in front of us. It was still fifty yards ahead of our boat, but it was finally close enough for me to see. And hear. As quickly as the tail had risen, it slammed back down to the water. There was a loud, low *thump* as it stunned its prey and slid beneath the surface. It was unfathomable. Majestic. Awe-inspiring. And a bit scary. We were a safe distance away, but I still wondered whether one of those whales might crush our boat. Still, we were too enthralled to move. For nearly ten minutes, we watched as they thrashed, dove, and fed. Bodies, fins, and tails paraded by in a fantastical water circus.

And then they were gone.

"If I had stayed home, we probably never would have seen them," said Katie.

I considered yelling, "See! I told you so!" or turning her words into some sort of lesson. Instead, I just nodded my head.

Sometimes our voyages do not pay off. It rained on our ski trip. The trip to Niagara was a bust. But, finally, here was an adventure that exceeded our expectations.

We continued to scan the horizon, but we never saw the whales again.

It was hard to believe we had actually observed them at all. We snapped no photos and recorded no video. We had been too far away at first, and then simply too excited. Luckily, families are one another's witnesses, repositories of curiosity, spectacle, and awe. We hold each other's memories in our hearts.

"Thanks for coming, sweetheart," I said to Katie. "This adventure was better because you were here."

We turned our boats around. With the sun setting over the ocean behind us, and the red nuns lined up before us, we paddled gently back to shore.

Conclusion: The Unfathomable Joy
of the Journey

In 1510, an unnamed cartographer created what has come to be known as the Hunt-Lenox Globe. It is a tiny copper sphere, depicting the artisan's best guess about what the world looked like at the time. The distant edges of the major continents are pure fantasy, sometimes appearing as smudges blurring into the sea. Whatever existed beyond the far horizon was unknown. In the great expanse of Pacific Ocean, off the coast of Asia, the mapmaker etched the words *Hic sunt dracones*: Here be dragons.

Though today's maps no longer bear images of dangerous creatures roaming the wilderness, families *still* feel compelled to travel well-worn paths. In our collective efforts to keep our kids safe, loved, and entertained, we raise them within trusted trade routes. We settle into the familiar rhythm of soccer in the fall, baseball in the spring, and just the right camps every summer. Before we know it, our children are on track for college or the workforce before they have ever had the chance to wonder, wander, or tame dragons.

There is nothing inherently wrong with occasionally joining the crowd or buying a family pass to Disney World. It is certainly easier.

But when we repeatedly follow a map around a theme park, when we routinely script our children's joy, we are taking something from them. All the paths are named. All the laughter is canned. We risk sending kids into the world without any *real* adventures, without ever having the chance to navigate open water.

Sometimes, the dragons our kids fear most become their greatest teachers. When we first moved to California, Katie was afraid of the homeless folks we often encountered. She avoided eye contact. She did not want to go to a popular burger joint because a man panhandled out front. But then we asked the gentleman his name, and we shared a simple meal. We listened to Eddie's story of his childhood in South Carolina and how he had landed in California after wandering across America. Katie learned empathy while talking with this stranger. She realized there was no dragon there.

While we do not always have time to share meals with people on the street, we have found other ways to serve. As a family, we have brought clothing and supplies to the women's refuge downtown. We have sold lemonade and cookies to raise funds for a local animal shelter. We have delivered meals to Family Promise, an organization committed to "ending homelessness one family at a time." We have taken to carrying granola bars in the car to share when we are confronted with a person in need.

Of course, sometimes, dragons are real. But rarely do they lurk over the horizon. Most wait silently in our path. Lizzie's surgeries were like that. They caught us in their clutches, monsters we could not avoid. But we fought them together, relying on reinforcements from family and friends, trusting one another in the face of challenges. In the end, Lizzie's scars healed, and we emerged stronger, more caring, and less afraid of the leviathans in wait. Whenever we encounter new challenges, we try to accept what they may teach us so that we might learn, grow, and discover those places where purpose and bravery come together.

That is perhaps the greatest lesson of all. In everything we have done, from counseling violent juveniles to bandaging wounded children, we have found that the closest thing to pure happiness occurs when service meets adventure. Before the kids, our lives were exciting and purposeful. With them, we have learned that wonder and worth are still possible. Parenting is difficult work, to be sure. Some days, we feel like selling the kids or maybe floating them out to sea. But in the fleeting moments when we glimpse the people our children are becoming, we cannot help but marvel at the contagiousness of their joy.

When Katie asks the lonely kid to sit at her lunch table, or when Lizzie invites an exchange student over to play after school, our kids prove that most purposeful acts do require a measure of bravery. Whether they are paddling toward a humpbacked whale or bringing barbecued chicken to a homeless family, when we see our children embody courage and service-mindedness, those are our proudest moments as parents. Days may be easier when we keep to set channels, but they are better when we wander off course, when we sail, hike, and drift into uncharted territories.

We are in our early forties now. Or, as Katie likes to say, "halfway to dead." In many ways, we have come full circle. Despite—or perhaps because of—our three children, we have discovered ways to view the world as something bigger than the needs of our little family. We are away from the kids from time to time. Ken's trips are occasionally longer than he would like, and Annmarie's are not long enough. But, as we discovered years ago, there is balance in the imbalance. Sometimes what we are doing today is worth missing our bedtime routines with the kids. Besides, it is okay to admit when we need help. And to retreat sometimes to safe harbors. When we do, we navigate in and out using our Nuns and Cans to guide us. We remember that true happiness is free, that even the worst storms end, and that it is always better when we can link our boats to others for safe passage through choppy water.

Some of our best adventures, and certainly the cheapest, are born of daydreams: the kind of wandering, rambling, full-of-possibility conversations that led the two of us to fall in love in the first place. Where will our next adventures take us? Fiji, Spain, Detroit? How can we best use our gifts? Politics, ministry, writing? What can we do together to make these aspirations a reality? We have had a few of these talks lately. We laugh about the mini regrets shared over the past twenty years—the mishaps, the misadventures, and even the harbors we were afraid to sail out of. Then we plot and scheme about the next twenty years—or the next fifty. We allow ourselves to be vulnerable together. We dare to believe that the best years are yet to come.

We will undoubtedly face more dragons. But worrying about them will not make us safer. And living inside the trade routes, never venturing into unknown waters, will not make us happier. Time and again, we discover that most of the monsters we invent for ourselves are as imaginary as those forewarned by the Hunt-Lenox Globe.

For half a millennia, mapmakers charting distant oceans imagined beasts roaming the unplumbed depths, lying in wait for any seafarer fool enough to stray off course. *Hic sunt dracones.* Most sailors heeded these warnings and remained content to ply the sea lanes. But others, the explorers and the wayfarers, looked to the unknown horizon. They saw the mapmakers' drawings not as portents but as invitations. Today, we follow in their wake. Here be dragons. *Come find them.*

References

Harvey, Jan, comp. 2011. "Factbox: Why are maternal deaths so high in Afghanistan?" Reuters. http://www.reuters.com/article/us-afghanistan-maternity-fb-idUSTRE7BB0FJ20111212 (accessed April 15, 2016).

Heintz, Kristin. 2007. "Two City Schools Labeled as Dropout Factories." YaleDailyNews.com. http://yaledailynews.com/blog/2007/11/06/two-city-schools-labeled-as-dropout-factories/ (accessed April 15, 2016).

Hrywna, Mark. 2016. "2016 NPT Best Nonprofits to Work: It's Fun, Games, Benefits and Serious Businesses at Top Nonprofits to Work." *The Nonprofit Times*. http://www.thenonprofittimes.com/wp-content/uploads/2016/04/4-1-16_SR_BestNonprofits.pdf (accessed April 15, 2016).

Topics and Questions
for Discussion

1. In the Introduction, Ken and Annmarie describe their Nuns and Cans, the beacons that guide their journey as parents. If you could pick a single Nun or Can that most influences your own approach to parenting, which one would it be? Is there one with which you disagree? As you reflect on your own parenting philosophy, is there a Nun or Can that you would add to the list?

2. In Chapter 1, Annmarie explains that her first impression of Ken was not a favorable one, and yet, by the end of the chapter, she talks about marrying him. What changed her mind? Have you ever been completely wrong about a person? When you look back on falling in love, can you remember that moment when you *just knew* you had met your match?

3. For the first seven years of their marriage, Ken and Annmarie chose not to have children. What are the pros and cons of such a choice? How should a couple go about deciding whether and when to have kids?

4. In Chapter 3, Annmarie describes the unexpected difficulties of being a new mother. What do you think is most challenging about becoming a parent?

5. Throughout the book, Annmarie describes how conflicted she is about working full time versus staying home. Have you or your partner ever experienced this tension?

6. When Annmarie and Ken lost their baby to a miscarriage, they did not have the benefit of a funeral or any kind of ritual to solemnize the loss. Do you think that rituals are important to the grieving process? Is there something that communities can do to help parents through the heartache of miscarriage?

7. In Chapter 8, during Lizzie's second surgery, Ken realized that the Harbaughs' emotional bulwark was, in fact, Annmarie. Do you respect him more for acknowledging his weakness? Or do you think fathers should always be a source of strength in a family? Who in your family do you lean on in a time of crisis?

8. In Chapter 9, Annmarie and Ken decide to wait for a natural childbirth with Henry. Do you think they made the right decision? Can you think of a time you decided you knew what was best for your children even though experts told you otherwise?

9. In Chapter 10, Ken describes his journey to the Philippines after a devastating typhoon. Upon his return, he finds it difficult to talk with Annmarie and the kids about his experience, but, ultimately, he discovers some solace in the sharing of it. How do you talk with your children about hard things while still helping them feel safe and loved?

10. In Chapter 11, Annmarie describes how all-consuming the job of a parent can be. Is it possible to be too devoted to one's family and children? When it comes to "changing your socks," do you agree with Ken and Annmarie that sometimes parents need to put themselves first? Why or why not?

11. Throughout the book, Ken describes occasions when he left his family for an extended period to fulfill professional obligations. What do you think of these absences? Should a career take precedence over time with family? What do you do to find balance with career and family needs?

12. Ken and Annmarie seem to understand a purposeful life as one that focuses on serving the wider world. Does finding purpose require looking outward in that way? Are there other kinds of purpose?

13. Throughout the book, Annmarie and Ken emphasize the importance of service, but in several chapters, they write about how

difficult it is to accomplish anything with children in tow. What opportunities have you found to serve in your community or in the larger world? Have you found a way to share these activities with your children?

14. Ken and Annmarie's love for one another seems to ebb and flow throughout the course of their marriage. In your experience, is that how love happens? Or do you believe true love is a more constant thing? What are the advantages and disadvantages of a relationship in which love evolves over time?

15. Much of Ken and Annmarie's parenting philosophy challenges the notion that the world is a dangerous place. *Seeking adventure . . . talking to strangers . . .* these ideas work fine if no one gets hurt. But as parents, how do we balance this positivity with the reality that sometimes there are actual dangers to be avoided? Can fear sometimes be a healthy attribute?

16. Over the course of their marriage, Ken and Annmarie move more than half a dozen times. What did you make of their frequent wandering? Did you respect their transience or find yourself wishing they would settle down? Are there safe harbors in your life that you sailed into but chose not to leave?

17. Why do you think Annmarie and Ken chose to call this book *Here Be Dragons*? What are the "dragons" to which they are referring? Can you point to any dragons in your life? Do you avoid them, tame them, or charge them head on?

ACKNOWLEDGMENTS

1. "OF COURSE YOU SHOULD WRITE A BOOK!"

Jimmy Soni, who gave us every writing break we've ever had.

Laura Yorke, our agent, who stuck with us through every "No" to find the right "Yes."

Ken Kurson, Sarah Kennedy, Mark Rykken, and the *New York Observer* team, for letting us tromp across the pages of their edgy paper with our stories about Vegas, sick kids, and lemonade stands.

Christopher and Michele Robbins, David Miles, Brooke Jorden, Erika Riggs, and the entire team at Familius, for taking a chance on alternating voice and the idea that a book by two parents writing together might be worth publishing.

Jessica Samakow, who gave us our very first pages on *HuffPo*.

2. "LEMME READ THAT BOOK!"

John Kelly, Rose Kelly, and Colleen deKeratry, for previewing our initial musings, for offering feedback, joy, and big questions, and for fixing our italicized commas.

The first wave of Team Dragons readers, advisors, and cheerleaders, in reverse alphabetical order (you're welcome, Ms. Zelenski), including, but not limited to: Jessica Zelenski, Jaya Vadlamudi, Rebecca Solovy, Alexis Rogers, Kate Oliver, Terri Mervenne, Melissa McCaverty, Jenny Kelly-Masloski and Scott Masloski, Kevin and Alex Kelly, Jennifer Jones, Kirk Jackson, Kim Harris, Kent and Ruth Harbaugh, Sarah Frauenzimmer, Eraina Ferguson, Jen Dotsey, Kelly Davis, Shannon Cooch, Emily Cherniak, David Callaway, Colby Barrett, and Doug Abdiel.

Our first endorsers, recommenders, and writer friends who were willing to lend us their names and mentorship to bring this book into the light: Katie Hurley, Jamie C. Martin, Joe Klein, Rev. Damian J. Ference, Kelly Watson, Tracey Miller-Zarneke, Julie Fishman, and Cecilia and Jason Hilkey.

All of the readers at DadvMom.com who have shared in our adventures and mishaps over the years.

3. "You're writing a book?"

Our parents, Kent and Kathy Harbaugh and John and Anna Marie Kelly, for teaching us to love unconditionally and for first instilling in us the joy of the journey.

4. Miscellaneous good people

Will McNulty and Jake Wood, for getting stuff done and for their vision in building the most purpose-driven nonprofit in operation today.

Eric Greitens and Chris Marvin, for their steadfast friendship and support.

All of Seabird Wave 1, including Ron Barry, Brian Brown, Breaux Burns, Elana Duffy, James McGreehan, Bob Obernier, Kate Oliver, Matthew Pelak, Kristen Rouse, Christopher Ryan, Lourdes Tiglao, Shane Valverde, and Chris "The Brit" Wharton.

All of Team Rubicon Nation, especially the staff and volunteers who have given Ken the most rewarding years of his professional life.

The teachers, students, campers, and chiefs who gave Annmarie courage, wisdom, and love, including, but not limited to, the folks at Camp E-Nini-Hassee, Eastside Catholic High School, West Ashley High School, and James Hillhouse High School.

You, for reading the whole acknowledgments page, which no one ever has, unless they are looking for their name and it's at the very end.

John Green.

About the Authors

ANNMARIE KELLY-HARBAUGH is a mother, teacher, and dog lover— an above-average cook and below-average housekeeper. Both a dancing queen and a brick house, she is an avid reader of cooking websites, fitness magazines, and articles that promise she'll lose weight fast. Annmarie earned a National Board Certificate in English Language Arts, holds a master's degree in urban education from Yale University, and has been a beloved teacher at half a dozen high schools from Florida to Seattle. She has taught Shakespeare to gang members and sung lullabies in a wilderness detention center. Annmarie's writing has appeared in the *Huffington Post*, in the *New York Observer*, and on National Public Radio.

KEN HARBAUGH has flown reconnaissance missions off North Korea, researched war crimes in Afghanistan, and deployed in response to natural disasters both at home and abroad. He cofounded The Mission Continues, an award-winning nonprofit that empowers military veterans to find purpose through community impact. He is currently the president of Team Rubicon Global, an organization that provides veterans around the world with opportunities to serve others in the wake of natural disasters. Ken's writing has appeared in the *New York Times*, the *Atlantic*, and the *Yale Journal of International Law*. He is not as funny as his wife.

Annmarie and Ken live in Los Angeles, CA, with their three children and an assortment of dying houseplants. Follow them at DadvMom.com, an online community dedicated to the proposition that couples can love one another and their children at the same time. Mostly.

About Familius

Visit Our Website: www.familius.com

Join Our Family: There are lots of ways to connect with us! Subscribe to our newsletters at www.familius.com to receive uplifting daily inspiration, essays from our Pater Familius, a free ebook every month, and the first word on special discounts and Familius news.

Get Bulk Discounts: If you feel a few friends and family might benefit from what you've read, let us know and we'll be happy to provide you with quantity discounts. Simply email us at orders@familius.com.

CONNECT:

www.facebook.com/paterfamilius
@familiustalk, @paterfamilius1
www.pinterest.com/familius

FAMILIUS

The most important work you ever do will be within the walls of your own home.

CPSIA information can be obtained
at www.ICGtesting.com
Printed in the USA
FSOW01n1848110816
23635FS